STAY WELL

How to keep he
the cold season
winter blues

By the same authors:
The Medicine Chest
The Pill Protection Plan

STAY WELL
IN WINTER

THE HEALTH AND NUTRITION PLAN TO PROTECT YOU AND YOUR FAMILY

Gillian Martlew, ND
and Shelley Silver

Illustrations by Gillian Martlew

THORSONS

THORSONS PUBLISHING GROUP

First published 1989

© THORSONS PUBLISHING GROUP 1989

Quote from *Watership Down* on page 5 copyright © 1972 by Richard Adams. Reprinted by permission of Penguin in the UK and Macmillan Publishing Company in the USA.

British Library Cataloguing in Publication Data

Martlew, Gillian
Stay well in winter: the health and nutrition
plan to protect you and your family.
1. Man. Health. Self-care
I. Title   II. Silver, Shelley
613

ISBN 0-7225-1850-1

Published by Thorsons Publishers Limited, Wellingborough,
Northamptonshire NN8 2RQ, England.

Typeset by Harper Phototypesetters Limited, Northampton
Printed in Great Britain by Richard Clay Limited, Bungay, Suffolk

1 3 5 7 9 10 8 6 4 2

Many human beings say
that they enjoy the winter,
but what they really enjoy
is feeling proof against it.

Richard Adams, *Watership Down*

CONTENTS

DEDICATION

For David, Cam, and Michael, who love the winter.
And for everyone who doesn't.

ACKNOWLEDGEMENTS

Our grateful thanks go to Valerie, for her usual thorough script reading. Love and thanks also to our families for their support. Additionally, our thanks go to Age Concern, Help The Aged, N.E.A., Jennifer Eastwood of SAD Association, and all the other groups and charities who provided us with invaluable help and information.

NOTE

The information contained in this book has been compiled as a result of careful review of medical and scientific literature, but it is not intended in any way as a substitute for the advice of a doctor, or to be used in place of medical care. No statement contained in this book shall be construed as a claim of cure or palliative for any condition of ill-health. Neither the authors nor the publishers accept any liability, however arising, from the use of any of the information contained herein, by any person whatsoever.

PREFACE

Winter is the time of year when the earth, plants, trees, and animals rest and conserve their energies for spring. It should be a time of slowed pace for us, but since the turn of the century, our lives have drifted away from the closeness we had with nature and the seasons. Less than 100 years ago, about a quarter of the population worked outdoors on the land, following the powerful dictates of the seasons — working hardest through spring, summer, and autumn, and slowing a little when nature proclaimed a time of rest in the winter.

Since divorcing ourselves from nature we have created artificial environments and lifestyles for ourselves. We live with concrete and tarmac, and our habitats have become houses, offices, shops, and cars. We are sealed in environments where the seasons are excluded, and in cities and large towns winter has become a time of ugliness, and inconvenience.

By shutting ourselves away from nature in an artificial environment, and by continuing to work at the same intensity through every season of the year, we have possibly upset an ancient circadian rhythm, and exposed ourselves to a lack of daylight and fresh air, a greater chance of cross-infection, and a multitude of man-made items that can make us feel ill and depressed. It is no wonder that by the time the days begin to draw in and we retreat into our homes, close the windows, and turn on the heating, we begin to feel mildly or even severely unwell, or we become more vulnerable to colds and infections.

This book aims to provide everyone in the family with the keys to health and happiness through the winter months. It is a comprehensive handbook for dealing with our newly adopted style of living; it outlines the problems and provides ideas for solutions. The whole family can learn the importance of the immune system, how to strengthen it, and how to eat healthy, warming, and healing winter foods. The book also includes some of the winter secrets that our great grandmothers knew, but which seem to have been lost in the shuffle of the last 100 years.

Chapter 1

FIGHTING THE COLD WAR

BODY HEAT

When icicles hang by the wall,
And Dick, the shepherd, blows his nail,
And Tom bears logs into the hall,
And milk comes frozen home in pail . . .

Shakespeare, *Love's Labour's Lost*

The winters in Shakespeare's Britain were much colder than they are now. The Thames froze and the winter climate was almost like a mini ice-age. By the early nineteenth century the winters were becoming warmer, and, although we still depict the Victorians' nostalgic snow scenes on Christmas cards, winters are now very much warmer, especially in the southern half of the country. However, winter in the British Isles is accompanied by a pervasive damp-cold which seems to 'chill us to the bone'.

In areas such as Canada and the north eastern United States, the temperature can plummet to many degrees below freezing.

The ideal internal temperature for an adult is approximately 98.6°F (37°C), although everyone's individual temperature varies slightly, and in children it may be a little higher because their temperature regulation is less precise. Women have a monthly cycle of temperature variation, characterized by a rise at the time of ovulation, and this is caused by increasing levels of the sex hormone progesterone.

HOW THE BODY REGULATES TEMPERATURE

We often complain of feeling cold in winter, but a healthy person's internal body temperature actually remains stable whether the environment is cold or hot. Even extremes like the heat of a sauna, and the cold plunge which follows, do not alter the internal temperature by more than 1°F. The body deals efficiently with these changes, because any prolonged alteration in the temperature could be dangerous or even fatal.

If our normal internal temperature decreases or rises about one degree, automatic cooling or heating mechanisms will be triggered, because even a slight drop in internal heat can slow biochemical reactions and affect mental alertness. If our environment cools, then messages from skin and organ-based sensors alert the body's thermostat in the hypothalamus. This activates involuntary nerve impulses which constrict blood vessels, moving them deeper into the skin so that heat is conserved. This way heat is maintained around the vital organs, although the skin feels colder. The simultaneous stimulation of involuntary muscle movement, shivering, produces warmth, and the contraction of muscles at the base of hairs in the skin causes goose pimples, raising the hairs and trapping a layer of warmed air next to the skin.

MAKING HEAT

We generate the equivalent heat of a 150 watt light bulb, and in one day we manufacture enough heat to boil a bath full of water.

Body heat is produced by cellular activity, breakdown of food, and muscular movement. The contraction of muscles uses energy and releases heat. We also receive warmth from external sources such as the sun, combustion, heating appliances, and proximity to other people.

Many centuries ago Aristotle thought that the heart made the body's heat and that it was 'a lamp fuelled by blood from the liver and fanned into spiritous flame by air from the lungs'. The heart is a muscle, and its contractions do produce some heat, but it is its pumping action that carries warm blood around the body and contributes most to body heat. As blood travels further away from the centre of the body, more heat is given up. This is why legs, feet, and hands are cooler than the torso. Although the lungs are a vital part of the cardiovascular system, heat is released whenever we exhale, and this can be felt by breathing on your hand. The loss of warm, moist air is one way in which extra heat is vented from the body, but in winter it can be a major cause of lost warmth.

FEVER

A fever is an abnormally high body temperature accompanied by shivering and a fast pulse. It is prompted when infectious disease or inflammation stimulates the production of a protein called endogenous pyrogen. This enters the brain and acts directly on the temperature regulating centre, in effect re-setting the body's thermostat to a new point above 98.6°. Temperature receptors then send messages that the body is too cold, and this activates mechanisms which produce extra heat. The sensation of chill during the early stages of a fever is produced by the retreat of blood vessels deeper into the skin leaving the surface of the body feeling cold. The shivering which also occurs is a sign that the body is stimulating the production of heat in order to increase the temperature to the new level.

Remedies to break a fever can be counter-productive because increased body heat stimulates the immune system, as well as directly destroying some of the invading micro-organisms. Bringing a temperature down can decrease the body's ability to fight the infection, and may prolong the illness. A fever which reaches 100-102°F is not harmful, but it is essential to consult a doctor if the temperature remains raised to 102°F or greater, causes severe discomfort, or lasts longer than three days.

If the temperature reaches 106°F the metabolism may become so rapid that the body's heat regulating mechanisms may have trouble returning to normal and the temperature will continue to rise. Cells begin to die at 108°F, and brain damage can occur. Even if the fever is reduced at this point, there may be permanent brain damage. A rise of another 4°F will usually result in death.

The three stages of fever

Stage one.   Fever develops and there is a sensation of chilliness with shivering. This may last between ten minutes to an hour. During this time the temperature can rise by approximately 2-4 degrees. As it climbs, metabolic activity rises and this is felt as an increase in heart-rate and pulse. This is followed by accelerated and deeper breathing as the body attempts to remove the by-products of increased metabolism.

Stage two.   This is the stage where the fever runs its course. The body feels hot and the temperature remains more or less constant at the new elevated level. There may also be headaches, sensitivity to light and cold, drowsiness, or restlessness. The body's cooling mechanisms are activated and blood flow to the skin increases to dissipate some of the body heat. The skin appears flushed, and the person feels hot. Plenty of fluid should be taken at this stage. Warm mineral water with a squeeze of fresh lemon juice, or home-made clear vegetable broth will help to replace lost minerals.

Stage three.   This is the final phase, when the fever breaks, and the body's thermostat returns to normal. Re-setting is triggered by the removal of the underlying cause, but if it still has a foothold in the body, the fever can return again.

Food and fever

The old saying, 'feed a cold, starve a fever', is partly correct. A person with a raised temperature, and therefore raised metabolism, should not be given solid foods. Plenty of warm liquid, with a squeeze of lemon, or vegetable broth are adequate and will not divert energy away from the healing process. Fever tends to reduce iron and zinc levels, but they should not be taken in supplement form during the temperature. It is believed that lowered levels of these minerals are necessary for the fever mechanisms to destroy the infection and an increased intake at this point may prolong the illness.

HYPOTHERMIA — THE CHILLING FACTS

Hypothermia may result if the body's internal temperature falls by 4°F. Respiration and heart-rate slow, blood pressure drops, and eventually consciousness is lost. Although hypothermia is not very common, it can be a danger for anyone exposed to extreme cold for an extended period of time. Being immobile in a cold room leads to a cooling of the body temperature, and for some elderly people, ageing may have brought about a decrease in the efficiency of the temperature regulating centre in the brain. It becomes more difficult to sense abnormal coldness, and the body may be less capable of maintaining its normal temperature in an extremely cold environment. Other particularly vulnerable groups include people who are undernourished, infants — especially newborn babies, diabetics, and anyone under the influence of drugs or alcohol. Cold can reduce alertness and reasoning and the victim of reduced body temperature becomes confused and helpless.

When the body's internal temperature reaches 28°C, its ability to return the temperature to normal spontaneously is lost. Slow re-warming is necessary to return the temperature to normal.

HELPING A VICTIM OF HYPOTHERMIA

If you are in contact with an elderly or house-bound person, be aware of the early symptoms of hypothermia which include shivering, pale skin, drowsiness, confusion, slurred speech, and slow breathing and pulse rate. If the body remains cold, then loss of consciousness will follow. An individual with hypothermia will have cold hands and feet, but a surer sign of hypothermia is a cold abdomen which is indicative of decreased internal body temperature. A standard thermometer does not register below 95°F (35°C), so there is the possibility that hypothermia can go unrecognized.

☑ Victims of hypothermia who are still conscious should be taken to a nearby doctor as quickly as possible. Wrap them warmly, but avoid bundling them in very heavy blankets or clothing which can decrease circulation. Do not turn the vehicle's heater up too high because it is important that the body is re-warmed gradually.

☑ If you do not have a vehicle, but the patient is still conscious, telephone for a doctor immediately. While you are waiting for professional help:

- Warm the room *slowly*.

- Offer the patient a warm (not hot or alcoholic) drink, but do not force it on them.

- It is very important to increase body heat *gradually*, so avoid using hot water bottles, electric blankets, or hot baths.

- The person should be lying down and covered with lightweight blankets. Resist piling very heavy blankets on top of the patient, as this can cut circulation and increase cold to the extremities.

- Be very gentle; avoid rubbing hands or feet vigorously.

☑ An unconscious patient should not be moved from the home except by a doctor or ambulance crew. Telephone for an ambulance immediately, and while you are waiting follow the procedure outlined in the previous paragraphs.

CLOTHES AND BEDDING

UTILIZING BODY HEAT

Scientists are developing clothing which will respond to changes in the climate by retaining heat in the cold, and releasing it when the temperature warms up. Thermal fabric is a product of the future, but we need to know the secrets of keeping warm using fabrics that are already available to us. Fabrics can be used to insulate the body from a cold or hot environment, but when it is cold some clothing and bedding materials are more efficient at retaining heat than others. The reason is that different fabrics have better insulating qualities and allow moisture from perspiration to vaporize.

Cloth fibres keep us warm by trapping air which has been warmed by the body, and this creates an effective barrier to heat loss. Several layers of light clothing and a garment lined with a light insulating material provide warmth by retaining body heat. Fishermen from the cold northern climates wear woollen jumpers knitted in patterns which create a number of layers within the garment, and these trap warmth. Usually the natural oils are left in the wool and this acts as an outer barrier against moisture and wind, while still allowing the skin to breathe, and perspiration to escape.

WINTER CLOTHES

Although everyone needs to dress appropriately for the cold, it is particularly important to clothe young children warmly, because they can become chilled very quickly. Anyone who is unable to lead an active life, or with certain medical conditions, may feel the cold easily; and as we get older the temperature-regulating mechanisms in the body tend to become a little less efficient, so some elderly people may feel very uncomfortable when the weather becomes colder and may need to wear extra warm clothing.

The best way to keep warm and comfortable is to dress in about three layers of natural fibre. Begin with a layer of cotton next to the skin. Thermal underwear is ideal because it allows perspiration to evaporate and traps two layers of warm air. To stop body heat escaping at the neck, wear a cotton polo neck shirt over the thermal underwear. For extra warmth, wear a wool cardigan or jumper, although this may not be necessary outside if you have a well-insulated jacket.

It is always important to keep the extremities warm, since these areas are naturally colder than the trunk of the body. Many people say that if their feet, head, neck, and hands are warm they feel warm all over. Wearing a hat helps to retain up to 20 per cent of body heat, and it is surprising how much warmer it can keep you. Body heat is also lost around the neck because warm air rises, so try wearing a silk or wool scarf to trap it. If you suffer from cold hands, wearing mittens can keep them warmer than gloves because there is a heat transfer from finger to finger rather than a heat loss when they are separated by gloves.

It is often a good idea to wear two layers of socks on a very cold day, especially if you get cold feet easily. Wear a thin pair of cotton socks next to your feet, and add a pair of wool socks on top. Make sure that your footwear accommodates the extra fabric comfortably, because tight-fitting shoes or boots reduce circulation and make feet feel cold no matter how many pairs of socks are being worn. Wearing tight footwear on a very cold day could also contribute to the development of chilblains due to restricted circulation. Warm your feet before going out on a cold day because they are likely to stay cold unless you will be walking very briskly or running.

When perspiration is trapped in shoes, both the socks and shoes become moist, and this makes feet cold, especially if you are standing. The best way to avoid this is to wear natural fibre socks, and avoid plastic or rubber footwear.

Similarly, avoid wearing a plastic or rubber-backed coat when you are very active. You are likely to perspire, even if it is very cold, and these garments prevent perspiration from being vaporized. This produces a high level of humidity close to the skin, which is uncomfortable, and will cool the skin quickly when you stop moving. Water conducts heat faster than air, so when clothing becomes wet it loses its insulating properties and actually increases heat loss. It is important to wear natural fabrics which allow perspiration to vaporize, and the ideal garment for cold, dry weather should be impermeable to wind, but still allow the skin to breathe. It should also trap a layer of warm air. A cotton jacket, lined with feathers or other bulky, but light, insulating material is ideal.

AND SO TO BED . . .

- A wool pad or a thick wool blanket placed under the bottom sheet will provide a thick layer of natural insulating material to hold body heat.

- Use 100 per cent cotton sheets and undersheets.

- Use a light duvet.

- Use a 100 per cent cotton duvet cover.

- Sleep in brushed cotton nightwear, or none at all if the room and bedding are warm.

The right bedding is as important as the right clothing in winter. We generally sleep for up to eight hours a day, and at this time the body is actively cleansing and eliminating waste through the skin and lungs. Sleeping in tight nightwear cuts circulation, and nylon or other synthetic fabrics are clinging and non-porous. The same is true of the actual bedding; nylon sheets are cold, do not allow your body to breathe, produce static, and are bad insulation, whereas brushed cotton sheets are just the opposite. If you wear nylon night-clothes, and sleep on nylon sheets, your movements will create a positive static charge and this may result in a bad night's sleep.

Heavy piles of blankets defeat their own purpose because their weight on the body cuts down circulation, and leaves you feeling colder. A light, insulating duvet can improve sleep and will retain heat by trapping the warm air rising from the body during sleep. As a result, the body remains at its own temperature through the night. In a warmth to weight ratio, a good quality duvet can provide up to four times more heat than blankets.

A WARM HOME

Making a few adjustments to keep the warmth in your home can add up to substantial savings on your power bills, and help to preserve the earth's ecosystem. A great percentage of heat is lost through the walls, roof, windows, and gaps around exterior doors, but proper insulation and draught-proofing can make a big difference in the amount of warmth you pay for, and the amount you actually live with.

See Chapter 11, under Energy — Help and Information, for details of how to get a free 'Monergy Pack'.

CHECKLIST 1   ARE YOU LOSING OUT ON WARMTH?

	✔	
1 Is the loft insulated to a depth of 4 inches (10cm)?		Up to 75 per cent of heat may be lost through a badly or un-insulated roof.

	✔	
1 Is the loft insulated? (cont.)		In Britain, if your home was built before 1975 and you have only 1 inch (2.5cm) of insulation, you may be able to claim for a grant to cover part of the cost of insulating to the recommended 4 inch depth. Contact your local DHSS office for information.
2 Are the doors and windows draught-proofed?		Heat loss through gaps in doors and windows can be substantial enough to warrant the cost of draught-proofing. Up to 25 per cent of your heating may be lost through single glazed windows. Place your hand round the edge of window and door frames. If you can feel a draught, cold air is entering the home and warm air is being sucked out.
3 Do your curtains hang *behind* radiators located under windows?		If your curtains hang *over* radiators when they are drawn, most of the heat will be directed out of the window. You may need to keep curtains drawn in cold rooms that you are not using, especially if there are large, north-facing windows.

	✔	
4 Have you put aluminium foil behind radiators located on outside walls?		The foil will reflect heat back into the room, preventing some of the loss through outside walls.
5 Have you moved furniture away from radiators for the winter?		Furniture placed in front of a radiator will block heat circulation and the heat may damage the furniture. Heat can also provide a conducive environment for dust-mites which live in upholstered furniture. People who have asthma or allergies are often allergic to dust-mites' waste products.
6 Have you installed nylon brushes at the bottom of exterior doors?		Brushes or metal strips prevent cold air from entering the building, and keep heat in the home.
7 Have you installed a draught-free letterbox flap?		On a cold day there can be quite a draught from the letterbox, and a significant loss of heat.
8 Are your hot and cold water pipes well insulated?		Insurance companies deal with thousands of claims for burst pipes in the winter. The water can cause extensive damage to the home and furnishings, and may even make the house uninhabitable for a period of time while repairs are being carried out.

	✔	
9 Is your hot water tank insulated with a 2 inch (7cm) thick cylinder jacket?		Heating water is one of the biggest expenses on your fuel bill. A non-insulated tank will cost money. If your tank is in an airing cupboard, line the walls with aluminium foil to reflect the heat back into the cupboard, especially if it is on an outside wall. In Britain, people with a low income and pensioners may be eligible for a grant to help cover some of the cost of a British Standard cylinder jacket. Enquire at your local DHSS office.
10 Have your boiler and gas fires been serviced for the winter?		If the heating appliances are inefficient you will have to pay more money for less heat, and they could be dangerous.
11 Has your chimney been swept lately?		Birds and small animals find chimneys very attractive for their housing. A nest could block the chimney, and soot and dirt decrease its efficiency and may increase the level of unhealthy combustion chemicals in the air.

HEATING AND VENTILATION

✔ It is important that all air vents in rooms remain open, as blocking them could result in a build-up of unhealthy chemicals in a room, especially if a gas, paraffin, or oil applicance is being used. For ventilation without draughts, talk to your local electricity board and enquire about trickle fans.

✔ If you are bothered by a draught from the floorboards, put newspaper under the underlay, then lay the carpet on top. Newspaper is a very good insulator but it should be removed or renewed after about three years as it will tend to disintegrate.

✔ Does your electricity or gas bill seem much too high? Contact the address on the bill as soon as possible and ask to speak to someone about it. If the bill is right, but you will have difficulty in paying it, it may be possible to arrange payments. If you are a pensioner, or are on a low income, contact the DHSS or Social Services, because you may be entitled to help. If you are threatened with cut-off, contact the fuel board immediately and explain your situation.

HELPFUL HINTS FOR A WARMER WINTER

✔ Live on the sunny side of your house and take advantage of free solar warmth.

✔ If the unoccupied rooms in your house are very cold, then on dull days close the curtains to insulate warmth.

✔ If you are elderly, ask someone to bring your bed into the living room or downstairs during winter's coldest months.

✔ Avoid putting your bed next to an outside wall. If possible locate it next to a warmer internal wall.

✔ Keep the bedroom temperature at about 60°F at night, and more if you are elderly. The ideal temperature for the living room is 70°F is you are elderly.

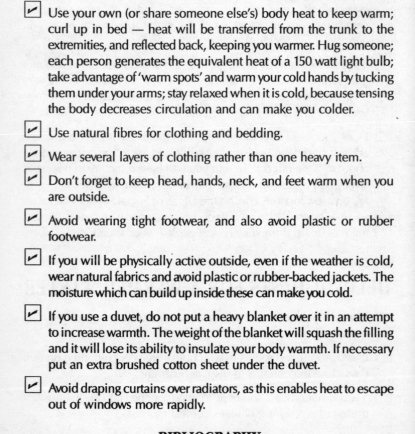

- ☑ Warm the bed before getting in — use an electric blanket, or a hot water bottle, but never use both together. Disconnect the electric blanket before getting in, unless you use an electric over-blanket.

- ☑ Use your own (or share someone else's) body heat to keep warm; curl up in bed — heat will be transferred from the trunk to the extremities, and reflected back, keeping you warmer. Hug someone; each person generates the equivalent heat of a 150 watt light bulb; take advantage of 'warm spots' and warm your cold hands by tucking them under your arms; stay relaxed when it is cold, because tensing the body decreases circulation and can make you colder.

- ☑ Use natural fibres for clothing and bedding.

- ☑ Wear several layers of clothing rather than one heavy item.

- ☑ Don't forget to keep head, hands, neck, and feet warm when you are outside.

- ☑ Avoid wearing tight footwear, and also avoid plastic or rubber footwear.

- ☑ If you will be physically active outside, even if the weather is cold, wear natural fabrics and avoid plastic or rubber-backed jackets. The moisture which can build up inside these can make you cold.

- ☑ If you use a duvet, do not put a heavy blanket over it in an attempt to increase warmth. The weight of the blanket will squash the filling and it will lose its ability to insulate your body warmth. If necessary put an extra brushed cotton sheet under the duvet.

- ☑ Avoid draping curtains over radiators, as this enables heat to escape out of windows more rapidly.

BIBLIOGRAPHY

Barbara R. Landau, *Essential Human Anatomy and Physiology*, Scott, Foreman and Company, 1976.

William F. Ganong MD, *Medical Physiology 10th Edition*, Lange Medical Publications, 1981.

Clayton L. Thomas MD, M.P.H. (Ed), *Taber's Cyclopedic Medical Dictionary* (15th Ed), F.A. Davis Company, 1985.

R.H. Fox et al. 'Body Temperatures in the Elderly: a National Study of Physiological, Social and Environmental Conditions', *British Medical Journal*, 27 Jan. 1973.

C.G.J. Bennett, 'Accidental Hypothermia', *Geriatric Medicine*, Feb. 1982.

Lee McManus, 'Cold Can Kill: the Facts About Hypothermia', *Self Health*, Sept. 1986.

K.J. Collins, 'Managing Hypothermia Patients at Home', *Geriatric Medicine* 12, Dec. 1986.

Age Concern, '*Owning Your Own Home*', July 1987.

Age Concern, '*Help With Heating Fact Sheet*', April 1988.

Age Concern, '*Warmth in Winter*', September 1987.

Help The Aged, '*Keep Warm This Winter*', 87/88.

Neighbourhood Energy Action, '*Fighting the Cold*'.

'Fabric with a difference', *New Scientist*, 31 July 1986.

Susan Smith Jones Ph.D., 'Clothing can Affect Your Health', *Health Express*, May 1983.

Chapter 2

IS YOUR IMMUNE SYSTEM TUNED FOR WINTER?

Winter is the season when health is often at its lowest ebb. It can be a time of frequent colds and flu, vague depressions, and general feelings of ill-health. Bacteria and viruses exploit the advantages that cold weather gives them, and although we are exposed to the same micro-organisms throughout the seasons, we tend to be more vulnerable to them in winter. Viruses need to penetrate our defence systems and invade cells in order to live and reproduce, and they find this easier when our immune system is not functioning in top condition.

> If ten people are exposed to the same stress factors, four may develop a cold, and six may not. The stress factors are the same, but the difference in susceptibility lies in the individual immune response.

One of the main reasons that some people seem more susceptible to illness than others is the strength of the immune response and its ability to cope with all the environmental, industrial, social, and domestic stresses and pollutants that we encounter each day. The immune system is a major key to health and when it is strong we are able to resist or overcome most of their effects.

In the winter we stay indoors longer, and are subsequently exposed to greater levels of chemicals from the products which surround us. There may also be low-level radiation from sources such as TV and VDU screens, some types of smoke detectors, cigarette smoke, nearby high-tension power lines, luminous clock and watch dials, satellite dishes, and natural radiation from rocks and soils in certain areas of the country. (See Chapter 4 for more information about low-level radiation.) If we are exposed to stress, pollutants, and low-level radiation to a degree which is intensive or prolonged, then their cumulative effects can weaken our immune resistance.

Other factors can influence our natural resistance to infection; for instance, during the winter, exposure to fresh air and sunlight is decreased and exercise is often taken less frequently. Anxiety and fear trigger the production of the hormones adrenaline and cortisol and when released in larger than normal amounts, and for prolonged periods, cortisol can suppress the efficiency of the immune system. On the other hand, a small increase enhances the immune response, so it is thought that a little stress is healthy.

We all need our immune system to function as well as possible in the winter, especially if we spend a large percentage of time indoors with other people. Heat encourages bacterial growth, and coughs and sneezes spread infections much faster in a warm atmosphere.

It is very important to be able to recognize whether or not your immune system is providing you with the degree of vital protection that it should be. The questions in Checklist 2 are intended to help you determine the level of your immune response. Check the key to find out how your immune system is coping.

CHECKLIST 2   EVALUATE YOUR IMMUNE SYSTEM

Group A	✔
Do you work or live in a city or heavily polluted area?	
Do you have more than one alcoholic drink every day?	
Do you drink more than one cup of strong coffee a day?	
Do you live or work in a very noisy area?	

Group B	✔
Do you eat a diet low in fresh wholefoods and high in refined and sugary foods?	
Do you smoke, or do you live or work with people who smoke?	
Do you frequently take prescribed or non-prescribed drugs?	
Do you regularly use drugs such as marijuana or cocaine?	
Are you exposed to very loud and continuous noise at your home or work?	
Do you live or work within 500 metres of high tension power lines?	
Are you a constant worrier?	
Are you experiencing emotional stress such as depression, grief/sorrow, anger or frustration?	

Group C	✔
Do you have food allergies?	
Do you have environmental allergies?	
Do you suffer from more than two colds or bouts of flu in a year?	
Do you suffer from frequent sore throats?	
Do you experience frequent cold sores?	
Do you suffer from thrush, fungal infections or yeast infections?	
Do you feel constantly fatigued?	

Key

Group A If you can tick 1–2 of the questions in group one, this indicates that your immune system is exposed to moderate levels of stress which could be affecting your immune response, especially in the winter when other factors combine to tax it. If you can tick more than two of the questions, your immune system is having to work quite hard to protect your health. Whatever your score, try to avoid these factors if you can, and for information about how to improve your immune response, see Chapter 3.

Group B Any of the situations in this group either alone or in combination, could be seriously affecting your immune function. Pressure on the immune system in the form of stress or environmental factors can limit or depress its protective ability, and exposure to viral or bacterial infection may result in illness. The risks tend to increase in winter weather, when we spend more time indoors, there is decreased exposure to fresh air and sunlight, and we get less exercise. All these factors combine to make us more vulnerable to infection.

If the factors which you have ticked are unavoidable in your life, then it is time to take some steps to help yourself before another winter takes its toll on your health.

See Chapter 3 for dietary suggestions that can help counteract the effects of environmental pollutants, and decrease some of the negative effects of stress.

See Chapter 11 for help with stopping smoking.

'A problem shared is a problem halved', and talking to a sympathetic friend, or a counsellor at the Samaritans, can be extremely helpful. If you regularly use drugs and would like some help or advice, contact:

UK
Release
169 Commercial Street
London E1 6BW
Daytime service (01) 377 5905
   24 hour emergency service (01) 603 8654

Release is an independent national agency concerned with the welfare of people using drugs, including people with legal problems over drug use. Release offers a confidential national service to drug users, dealing with illegal and prescribed drug use, drugs and the law, and general legal problems.

Alternatively, telephone the operator and ask for *Freephone Drug Problems*. A recorded message will give a telephone number to contact for every county in England, Wales and Scotland.

This association is the national co-ordinator for drug services in the UK and it provides advice on local services for people with drug problems.

USA
National Institute for Drug Abuse
5600 Fisher's Lane
Rockville
Maryland 20857
Telephone (301) 443 6720

Group C If you have ticked any of the questions in this group then your immune system is showing visible signs of stress. Follow the suggestions in Chapter 3, and throughout the book you may find clues to the triggers of the disorder.

For individual help you may wish to consult a naturopath, clinical ecologist, homoeopath, herbalist or acupuncturist.

QUICK REFERENCE IMMUNE SYSTEM RESPONSE CHART

◀ DECREASED	INCREASED ▶	FACTOR
	▶	Balanced diet
	▶	Daily diet containing fresh wholefoods
◀		Exposure to low-level radiation

◄ DECREASED	INCREASED ►	FACTOR
◄		Exposure to loud, continuous noise
◄		Exposure to pollution
	►	Exposure to sunlight
◄		Exposure to tobacco smoke
◄		High intake of alcohol
	►	High intake of fried food or saturated fats
	►	High intake of sugar, starches, and refined foods
◄		Inadequate sleep
◄		Poor nutrition
	►	Regular exercise
	►	Relaxation
◄		Severe or prolonged stress
◄		Taking large doses of corticosteroid drugs

HOW THE BODY FIGHTS INFECTION

The immune system is a very complex army of cells which come to our rescue whenever viruses, bacteria or other micro-organisms infect our bodies.

We live in a world surrounded by micro-organisms, and many of these need us in order to live and reproduce. Our first line of defence against these unwelcome guests is the skin — it produces fatty acids which are toxic to many micro-organisms. Areas such as our eyes, mouth, lungs, and digestive tract are more vulnerable but they have their own systems of defence; secretions such as tears, sweat, urine, and saliva contain an enzyme called muramidase which can kill certain types of bacteria. Mucus in the nose and airways prevent bacteria from penetrating the mucous membranes, and tiny 'hairs' called cilia push the mucus out of the airways into the throat where it is swallowed and the organisms are killed by the acids in the stomach.

In the intestines, bacteria known as the 'gut flora' help to exclude harmful microbes and take up spaces where they could grow. Vaginal secretions are hostile to viruses, bacteria, and fungi because they contain lactic acid which is produced when helpful bacteria feed on a carbohydrate excreted by the vagina. See Chapter 11 for information on contacting a natural practitioner in your area.

If micro-organisms penetrate these first lines of defence, the body has the difficult task of identifying them as invaders and dealing with them without damaging its own cells. All the cells in the body have special 'chemical markers' on their surfaces which prevent the immune system from attacking them. Viruses, bacteria and other invaders are also chemically marked, and this is how the body tells the difference between them.

The white blood cells or leucocyte's consist of phagocytes, macrophages, and granulocytes which scavenge and destroy organisms. Red blood cells outnumber white cells 500:1.

Leucocytes are a vital part of our immune systems and they travel in the blood and in the lymph system, which is a vast network of vessels found throughout the body. Part of the lymph system's function is to carry invading organisms from the site of infection to the nearest lymph glands where lymphocytes and leucocytes will kill them. Lymph glands are located throughout the body, particularly in the neck and throat, under the arms, near the large veins in the abdomen, and in the groin region. You may notice 'swollen glands' in these areas when the body is actively fighting an infection. The lymph and debris then passes into the bloodstream to the spleen where final processing is performed.

While this is happening, the chemical markers (antigens) from the invading organisms are identified and the B-cells in the lymph nodes manufacture antibodies. These are special chemical weapons which will also attack the organisms, making it easier for the scavenger white blood cells to dispose of them. When their work is completed, antibodies remain in the body as blueprints so that, if exposed to the same organisms again, the body can quickly manufacture the right weapons to render them harmless. This is known as immunity, and an example is the unlikely event of suffering from chickenpox again if you were exposed to it during childhood. Antibodies are also manufactured after exposure to antigens in vaccines and this can also produce immunity.

The thymus gland, spleen, and tonsils are also very important components of the immune system and they produce and stimulate lymphocytes and antibodies.

VIRAL INFECTIONS

A viral infection such as influenza is spread from one person to another in the water droplets which escape during sneezing and coughing. It is also passed around through hand contact and transference to objects such as door handles.

If the virus penetrates the mucus defence in the nose and upper part of the respiratory tract, then it may spread to the lungs and become an infection. Once viruses have a foothold they begin to reproduce in our cells. There is an incubation period of one or two days before the unpleasant symptoms of an infection begin to appear. As microbes multiply, they use nutrients and oxygen meant for the body's own cells, and the waste substances they produce are harmful to body tissues.

A viral infection, and how the body fights it
The diagrams on pages 38-41 show how your defence system works.

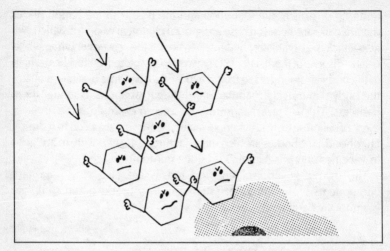

Invading organisms manage to penetrate the body's first lines of defence. Once inside the body they take over cells in order to live and reproduce.

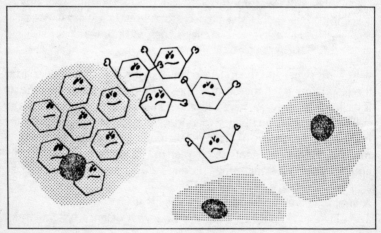

As the number of viral organisms increases, the invaded cell bursts and releases the viruses which then invade other cells.

Phagocytes constantly patrol the body, and are the first to encounter the invading organism. Granulocytes are phagocytes which destroy organisms by engulfing them and exposing them to granules of chemicals.

Macrophages (big eaters) are also phagocytes, and are known as the body's main refuse collectors. They engulf and digest stray viruses and display a piece from the invader called an antigen. This alerts helper T-cells.

Helper T-cells are lymphocytes which detect antigens and send urgent chemical messages to their cousins, the killer T-cells. The chemical messages hurry killer T-cells to the site of infection and enhance their action.

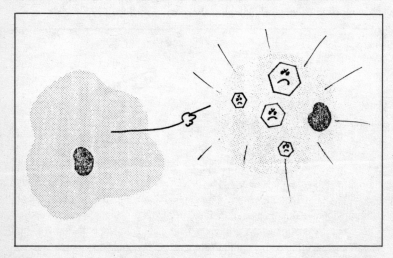

Killer T-cells prevent the viruses from multiplying by puncturing the membranes of cells which they have taken over. In the process these cells are destroyed and macrophages clean up the debris.

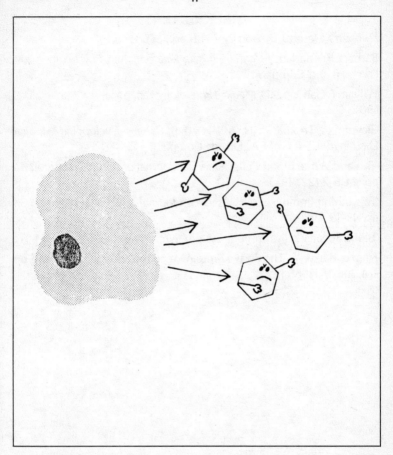

B-cells remain dormant in the lymph glands until alerted that antigens are present. B-cells produce antibodies, chemical weapons, which damage the invading organisms and make it easier for the phagocytes to dispose of them. After an infection antibodies remain as 'blueprints' and if the same viruses or bacteria come along again, the body quickly produces the right defences. This time you may not even be aware of the new exposure to the organism, or you may only experience a transient or minor reaction.

BIBLIOGRAPHY

Dorland's Medical Dictionary, (24th ed), Saunders.

Barbara R. Landau, *Essential Human Anatomy and Physiology*, Scott, Foreman and Company.

William F. Ganong MD, *Medical Physiology*, Lange Medical Publications, 1981.

Clayton L. Thomas MD, M.P.H. (Ed), *Taber's Cyclopedic Medical Dictionary* (15th ed), F.A. Davids Company.

'Fats and White Blood Cells', *American Journal of Clinical Nutrition* 32, pp. 2416–2422, 1979.

'Fats Inhibit Immune Cells', *American Journal of Clinical Nutrition* 33, pp. 13–16, 1980.

'Blood Sugar and the Immune System', *Nutrition Review* 40, pp. 161–171.

Frances Balkwill, 'The Body's Protein Weapons', *New Scientist* 1617, pp. 1–4, Jun 16, 1988.

Chapter 3

WINTER FOOD POWER

Food can be warming and healing, and it has the power to increase or decrease health or immunity. Knowing how to choose the right food and drink for all the family can provide a strong foundation for protection against winter ailments while they are making their annual rounds.

The body needs a balance of carbohydrates, proteins, fats, vitamins, and minerals to function properly, and the right diet also provides nutrients which the immune system needs to stay strong. A diet which includes as much variety as possible helps to ensure that there are no nutritional gaps, and it is also important to know where the gaps can occur. Different age-groups and different dietary preferences all need to be looked at in order to choose the right winter diet.

VEGETARIANS AND VEGANS

Everyone needs to make sure that enough vitamin D-rich foods are included in the diet during the winter, but some vegetarians and vegans need to be especially careful. Sunlight's ultraviolet rays produce vitamin D by the conversion of a form of cholesterol which is found under the skin. During the winter months, our exposure to sunlight decreases, especially from December to early April, and as a result the main source of this nutrient becomes the diet. Dairy products, oily fish such as mackerel, herrings, sardines and salmon, egg yolk, margarine, and liver are the richest dietary sources.

Some vegetarians and vegans may become deficient in vitamin D during the winter because dietary intake of this nutrient, and sunlight, are very limited.

If you, or members of your family, avoid all animal foods and rely solely on vegetarian margarine for your source of vitamin D in the winter, check that you are using a brand which does not contain hydrogenated oils. These are highly saturated and are not healthy for either the cardiovascular or the immune system.

Vegan children may be at risk of faulty bone formation if, while they are growing, their vitamin D levels are inadequate. Vitamin A levels may also suffer in the winter if fruit and vegetables are the primary source of this nutrient. Excellent sources of pro-vitamin A include dark green vegetables, orange and yellow fruit and vegetables. For extra vitamin A, serve steamed, organic beet leaves, organic carrot tops, and fresh dandelion leaves from a non-polluted source. Unless there is sufficient intake of vitamin D, or exposure to full spectrum light, women who avoid animal foods may suffer more severely from menstrual cramps, and after the menopause, osteoporosis may be more likely to occur.

Taking certain prescription medicines can decrease the absorption of vitamin D, or increase its requirements. To find out whether you are taking any medicines that affect this vitamin, see Chapter 9.

For those who are concerned that they, or other family members, may become deficient in vitamin D during the winter because of dietary choice, it is possible to 'supplement' vitamin D by installing full spectrum light tubes in the home and workplace; see Chapters 6 and 11.

People who become vegetarian or vegan after eating meat for most of their lives often complain that they feel colder in the winter since the change in their diet. The reason for this may be that the intake of iron and B12 drops with the discontinuation of meat. Iron can be supplemented naturally by taking *Floradix* liquid which is a mixture of herbs, vegetables, yeast, and fruit. Foods containing B12 can be found in the Immune Nutrients Quick Reference Chart in this chapter. Meat also has a stimulating effect on the system, and when this is withdrawn people often complain of feeling tired and colder.

THE ELDERLY

The ageing process can bring about a decline in the way our bodies assimilate and utilize nutrients, especially minerals. For this reason it is important to make sure that the diet supplies nutritious and easily digested foods. During the winter, intake of fresh fruit and vegetables tends to be lower than in the summer months and there is often a heavier reliance on starchy foods, stews, and puddings. Because of this, there may be a decline in the amount of vitamin C available in the diet.

Recent studies show that elderly men need even more daily vitamin C than women and during the winter, when intakes may be lower and stress levels can be high, it is important to meet a minimum maintenance requirement of at least double the RDA of 60mg. A supplement containing 250mg of vitamin C with bioflavonoids can be taken safely once a day, and will contribute to a healthier immune system.

Vitamin D is especially important for anyone who spends most of the winter indoors. Vitamin D is inolved in the body's utilization of calcium and phosphorus. Softening of the bones, muscle weakness, and pains or spasms in the limbs are deficiency symptoms. The instance of brittle bones may be less common in later life if there is enough vitamin D, calcium, and magnesium available in the diet, in conjunction with a little more exercise. See under Vegetarians and Vegans in this chapter for food sources of vitamin D. For sources of calcium and magnesium, see the Immune Nutrients Quick Reference Chart in this chapter.

If dietary choices limit the amount of vitamin D, then the alternative option is to install full spectrum light tubes in the home, especially since it is often difficult to go outside when the weather is particularly cold, wet, or windy. See Chapters 6 and 11 for more details.

Vitamins A and D work in conjunction with each other, and are usually found together in foods of animal origin such as oily fish, fish liver oil, and dairy products. Vitamin A is important for the health and immunity of the respiratory system and the mucous membranes. If the diet is lacking in yellow, orange, and dark green vegetables, or if fish and dairy products are not eaten very often, it may be necessary to take some supplementary cod liver oil or fresh oil capsules to protect against frequent 'chesty colds'.

CHILDREN

Children's insatiable love-affair with sweets and sweet foods can make them more vulnerable to winter infections because a high intake of sugar can lower the immune response. Given the exposure to cross-infection during school hours, especially when the classroom heating is on, it is important for the immune system to be strong, otherwise frequent colds and runny noses can make winter miserable.

It is usually very difficult to make sure that children always eat well, especially when they are at school. Try to make sure that whenever children eat at home, the diet consists of wholefoods with plenty of fresh fruit and vegetables. Packed lunches can be made more appetizing by including fruit-juice sweetened biscuits and cakes, 'live' yogurt with fruit-juice sweetened jam for flavouring, plenty of fresh and dried fruit, and fresh vegetables such as raw carrots, sprouts, celery, and red cabbage. For a special treat include some sprouted grain 'Manna' bread which is becoming more widely available in health and specialist food stores.

MEDICINES AND NUTRIENTS

If medicines are being taken long-term, or if a number of different prescriptions are used at the same time, nutrient deficiencies may occur, especially if the diet is inadequate. The elderly may be especially vulnerable to nutrient depletion, and this can affect the efficiency of the immune system.

See Chapter 9 to find out whether any medicines you are currently taking may be increasing your need for any specific nutrients. Use the information that follows in this chapter to ensure that your diet provides all the vitamins and minerals you need.

GETTING THE MOST FROM YOUR DIET

It is possible to increase nutrient absorption by chewing all foods well, and choosing foods and food supplements that will supply nutrients in the most effective way. The following points will help you to find out how to get the most from your diet, eat warming foods, and avoid dietary habits which could be robbing your body of the very nutrients it needs to stay warm and healthy.

- ✔ Natural food supplements such as fresh wheatgerm and rice bran are high in vitamins and minerals which are important for general health and the health of the immune system. When added to food, they increase the nutrient content of any meal. Sprinkle up to a tablespoonful of wheatgerm and/or ricebran on meals, once or twice a day. Always buy wheatgerm or ricebran which are vacuum sealed by the manufacturer, and when they have been opened, store them in the refrigerator. Avoid eating them if there is a rancid smell or a strong 'burning' taste.

- ✔ Mint herbal tea warms the body, and other warming foods include ginger which can be grated fresh into cooking, Japanese diakon radish, and hot soups with added sea vegetables. Avoid spicy foods such as curries because they cause you to perspire and cool you down; this may be the reason why they are favoured in hot countries.

- ✔ Chew a teaspoonful of linseeds before each meal to improve digestion and elimination, and provide essential fatty acids.

- ✔ You can add a concentrated source of nutrients to your daily diet by grinding two tablespoons each of sesame, sunflower, and pumpkin seeds into a meal. Sprinkle a teaspoonful of the seed meal into your salad or yogurt for a digestible source of calcium, zinc, fatty acids, protein, and other nutrients. Store the seed meal in a glass jar in your refrigerator to prevent the oils becoming rancid.

- ✔ When blood levels of haemoglobin are normal, and if circulation is good, there is less likelihood of extreme sensitivity to the cold. Ensure that plenty of iron-rich foods are included in the diet, and for more information, see the food chart in this chapter.

- ✔ Thicken soups, gravies, and casseroles with kuzu root powder, obtainable from specialist shops. The starch is easy to use and is less refined than cornflour or potato starch. Kuzu is used in oriental medicine to soothe gastro-intestinal irritation and diarrhoea.

✔ It is important to balance your intake of cooked food with plenty of raw foods, and include fresh seasonal vegetables such as cabbage, sprout tops, and leeks. Fresh and raw foods are essential to health in the winter when a large proportion of the diet consists of cooked meals. Uncooked fresh foods provide the body with enzymes and nutrients which may be missing in cooked, packaged or frozen foods.

Grate two large raw carrots and half a beetroot and eat a third of the mixture with each meal. Raw beets and carrots provide enzymes, nutrients and fibre, and are more easily digested when grated.

If you are unused to raw vegetables, use only half the quantity suggested and gradually increase it over a period of a week or two. If you are unable to tolerate raw vegetables begin by steaming them well, and over a period of time gradually reduce the cooking time until you can eat them raw, or almost raw.

Always try to buy organically grown vegetables if you can, because a high intake of foods containing agricultural chemical residues may lower the immune response in some individuals.

Fruit should be eaten raw but if this is not tolerated, it can be lightly stewed in water with a little concentrated fruit juice, or a small amount of raw honey or date syrup for sweetening. Cloves, cinnamon, and ginger can be added to provide a pleasant flavour, and for their antiseptic and warming oils.

✔ Drinking copious quantities of tea and coffee robs the body of B vitamins and iron. Drinking a cup of tea with a meal blocks the absorption of iron which is important for immune function, and for staying warm. Coffee also inhibits iron absorption, although not as severely as tea. Even decaffeinated coffee limits iron absorption because this effect seems to be due to the iron-binding capabilities of polyphenols which are found in both types of coffee.

If you are a heavy consumer of coffee and would like to decrease your intake, do not stop it immediately as it could make you feel very weak, cold, bad-tempered and over-emotional. Stimulants such as caffeine affect the metabolism and the adrenal glands, and it is very important not to withdraw caffeine from the diet too quickly.

To gradually decrease your intake of coffee, try the following:

Week one — use a quarter of a teaspoon less of your regular coffee and replace it with a quarter of a teaspoon of grain or dandelion coffee substitute. Continue this for a month while your body becomes used to the decreased level of caffeine, and you become accustomed to the taste.

Week four — cut the regular coffee down to half a teaspoon, and add half a teaspoon of coffee substitute; continue with this for a month.

Week eight — reduce the regular coffee to a quarter of a teaspoon and add three quarters of a teaspoon of coffee substitute. Continue with this amount of coffee until you feel able to switch entirely to coffee substitute.

Tea can be reduced more easily and is best done by substituting one or two daily cups of regular tea with rooibosch (red bush tea), or a herbal mixture that you enjoy.

☑ Alcoholic drinks may make you feel warmer initially, but alcohol can make you colder because it opens up the blood vessels, causing your body to lose heat rapidly. Alcohol also increases your need for B-complex and zinc, two vital nutrients for the immune system. However, a very small glass of wine or an occasional small alcoholic night-cap is unlikely to be too detrimental. Alcohol can increase the side-effects of some medications, and could make you feel colder; see Chapter 9 for information about drugs and winter.

☑ Avoid smoking or smoky atmospheres whenever possible. Medical studies show that smoking decreases circulation to the extremities and can make you feel colder, especially if you have a sedentary lifestyle.

☑ If you feel a cold coming on, avoid sugar in all forms for a few days as it can decrease immune response. Eating large quantities of refined white sugar also increases your need for the mineral chromium which is required by the infection-fighting white blood cells. Other foods that should be avoided in excess are white flour and fatty foods.

✓ Yogurt should be included in the daily diet because it contains easily-digested protein, and calcium. Yogurt helps to feed the intestinal bacteria which, in turn, aids digestion, elimination, and the immune system.

✓ Bottled or packaged fruit drinks that are high in sugar, colouring and preservatives can be immunosuppressive. Choose natural, unsweetened juices, or better still, make your own from fresh fruit. See Immune Boosting Drinks in this chapter.

✓ Cook foods with care to preserve their nutrients. Avoid adding bicarbonate of soda to vegetables, avoid excessive heat, cut vegetables as little as possible before cooking, keep pans covered to prevent the loss of nutrients in steam, and try not to soak vegetables before cooking them. See Immune Nutrients Quick Reference Chart for information about what destroys specific vitamins and minerals.

✓ Kelp powder can be sprinkled on food to increase its iodine and trace-mineral content. Iodine is an important mineral for the thyroid gland which is involved in metabolism and keeping warm. If your diet is low in iodine, then consuming large quantities of foods which can have an anti-thyroid effect may contribute to lower tolerance of cold weather. Goitrogenic foods include cabbage, cauliflower, kale, turnips, soybeans, carrots, and Brussels sprouts. Including kelp, fish and seafoods in the diet helps to counteract this effect.

NOTE: If you are taking any medicine for your thyroid gland, do not increase your intake of iodine unless directed to do so by your doctor. Too much iodine could dangerously increase or decrease your medicine's effect.

✓ Garlic's power to keep colds and infections at bay is not to be sniffed at. Garlic is rich in a sulphur-containing amino acid called alliin. When crushed it is converted to allicin which has a strong smell, and potent antiviral and antibacterial properties. You can use 1–3 cloves a day or, if this also keeps friends at bay, try taking 1–2 garlic capsules instead.

✔ Even if you do not feel thirsty, it is important to include plenty of liquids in the diet to prevent the danger of dehydration. These can include soups, herbal teas, warm water with a squeeze of lemon, fruit juices, soy milk, goat and other milk, coffee substitutes. Individuals who are dehydrated in extremely cold weather can be up to 20 per cent colder than normal. The water vapour lost during breathing accounts for loss of liquid, and cold weather often increases the urinary output.

✔ A steaming bowl of porridge oats provides a warm start to the day. Oats contain a healthy soluble fibre which helps to lower harmful cholesterol in the blood. Excessive cholesterol in the blood vessels may be responsible for impeding circulation, and may lead to heart disease.

✔ Avoid uncooked wheat bran; it can rob your body of vital minerals, especially zinc, and it may make you constipated when used in large quantities. A better, and tastier, way to increase your dietary fibre is to eat wholegrain foods, oatbran, fruit, and vegetables.

✔ Whenever possible, eat fresh, or stewed fruit rather than sweet snacks. Try not to fill up with cakes and biscuits — they are generally low in fibre, high in sugar, and provide little nutrition.

✔ If you are alone, and find that you have stopped cooking proper meals for yourself, have you thought of getting together with friends to take it in turns to make meals? It can be uplifting to be with friends and it is a healthy challenge to make a meal for other people.

✔ Opting for a healthy, balanced diet need not be too expensive. There can be more room in the budget for better foods if meat is kept to a minimum. Cheese, egg, vegetable, and bean-based meals can be substituted. Fish is inexpensive, easy to cook and very digestible. Try baking or steaming it rather than frying.

✔ A nourishing bowl of soup can be made with yeast extract or vegetable stock, and left-overs. Also add an onion, lentils, grated fresh ginger root, and some root vegetables.

NUTRIENTS AND THE IMMUNE SYSTEM

Vitamins, minerals, and other food components are very much involved in the way the immune system functions. A balanced wholefood diet is an important aspect in the health of the immune system, but too much of a specific food or nutrient can be as immunosuppressive as too little, especially for the elderly. If supplements are taken they should work together synergistically, and small doses taken 2–4 times a day are much more effective than large doses of single nutrients. Vitamins and minerals enhance cellular immunity by preventing cell damage and strengthening cell walls so that they are more able to resist disease. Nutrients can directly affect the production of white blood cells, lymphocytes, and antibodies which are the body's cell-mediated defences. More information on the immune system can be found in Chapter 2.

- **Calcium** helps to maintain strong cell walls which can resist viral penetration, and it activates enzymes that are important for stress response and fighting viral infections. The body's need for this mineral increases greatly during a viral infection. Vitamin F, found mainly in oils, seeds, wheatgerm, and nuts, helps to make calcium available to the tissues.

- **Choline**, a member of the B-complex vitamins, is required for healthy and strong cell membranes. The body also uses choline to produce DMG (dimethyl glycine) which enhances oxygen uptake, immune response, and antibody production.

- **Chromium** is required for the immune system's white blood cells. It is lost from the white cells during stress, so the diet should contain plenty of this mineral in order to maintain a strong immune response.

- **EPA** (eicosapentaenoic acid), which is found in fish oils, appears to have the ability to activate the immune system.

- **Folic acid** is a B-complex vitamin which is needed for the production of white blood cells. Deficiency of this nutrient can inhibit antibody production.

- **Fat** can suppress immune function when eaten in large quantities, especially saturated fat from sources such as meat, cream, cheese, hydrogenated oils etc. EPA (see above) can have a positive effect. Rancid fats can damage cells and make it easier for viruses to penetrate them and multiply. A diet high in polyunsaturated fatty acids appears to be immunosuppressive.

● **Germanium** is a naturally occurring mineral compound which research has shown to be a very effective immunostimulant. Its positive effects on health were discovered by a Japanese metallurgist, Dr Kazuhiko Asai, while he was carrying out research into germaniun in coal. One of germanium's main qualities is its ability to aid the body's utilization of oxygen which is a vital key in cell and tissue health. It may help people suffering from allergies that result from abnormal antibody production — a disorder which can also affect immunity. Germanium is effective against viral infections, and can increase resistance to flu viruses. Germanium enhances the body's production of interferon, a special type of protein which impedes viral attack on cells, and it enhances the effects of white blood cells. Germanium is found in significant quantities in garlic, comfrey, aloe vera, ginseng, and suma. The germanium content of garlic and ginseng is partly the reason why these herbs are protective against viral infection.

Supplements of germanium are available, although they are relatively expensive. If you decide to take supplements of this mineral, ensure that it is organic germanium, (Dr Asai's special form of germanium, carboxyethylgermanium sesquioxide — GeOxy-132). To gain the most benefit take approximately 60mg, under the tongue, up to four times a day, unless advised otherwise by a doctor or natural practitioner.

● **Iron** works with copper, folic acid and B12 to prevent anaemia. A condition of iron depeletion, which may not even show up as anaemia, can be enough to depress immunity. On the other hand, too much iron can increase the disease-causing ability of micro-organisms, so it is best to ensure that the diet contains plenty of iron-rich foods. If you feel it may be necessary to take iron supplements, contact your doctor or a natural practitioner for advice. See Chapter 11 to find out about contacting a practitioner in your area.

- **Potassium** acts as an ascorbate transporter, aiding in the entry of vitamin C through cell membranes where it aids the process of immunity.

- **Protein** helps to move vitamin A stores from the liver into the bloodstream, and acts as a transporter, aiding in its release. Protein is composed of a number of amino acids which the body uses to make antibodies, lymphocytes, and macrophages. Amino acids are also used by the body to make lymphokines, the substances released by lymphocytes during contact with specific antigens, and which help to produce immunity by stimulating certain white blood cells.

- **Selenium** enhances the immune response, and contributes to the formation of the body's protective protein, interferon. When selenium is taken with vitamin E, it is involved in the production of antibodies.

- **Vitamin A** promotes the growth and repair of tissues; it is necessary for the production of antibodies and white blood cells, and is known as the anti-viral vitamin. By helping to keep cell walls strong, and maintaining the mucous membranes, vitamin A also helps the body to prevent viruses and other micro-organisms from gaining a hold in the body. It is a vital nutrient for the health of the respiratory system and can help to prevent respiratory infections. As the temperature drops, the liver tends to release less of its store of this nutrient and its metabolism is inhibited, so it is important to include plenty of vitamin A sources in the diet, and to eat enough zinc-rich foods because zinc helps to mobilize vitamin A reserves. Beta carotene, from vegetables and fruit, activates helper T-cells and promotes improved immunological function. Supplemental doses of more than 10,000–25,000iu of vitamin A taken daily over a period of time can have a negative effect on immunity by prematurely liberating enzymes from white blood cells and macrophages which then attack and damage cells. Anyone with liver or kidney disorders should avoid taking large daily doses of vitamin A, except under supervision. Many people in the UK may be taking vitamin A in the winter, and a daily supplement of carotene or fish liver oil may be necessary to maintain the health of the immune system and the mucous membranes.

- **Vitamin B1** is immunity maintaining, especially in conjunction with vitamin C, and the amino acid L-cystine.

- **Vitamin B2** is important for the maintenance of the mucosal barrier, one of the body's first lines of defence against invading micro-organisms. It works with the other B vitamins, B5, B6, and folic acid, to promote antibody production.

- **Vitamin B3** is needed by the body for the health of cells and tissues, and it may have a moderate effect on antibody response.

- **Vitamin B5** is involved in the production of antibodies, and of the adrenal hormone, cortisone, which in normal quantities can influence the production of white blood cells and antibodies.

- **Vitamin B6** is necessary for cell multiplication and is needed for good antibody and white blood cell response.

- **Vitamin C** has gained quite a controversial reputation as the 'cure' for the common cold. It does, however, have a vital role to play in the immune system, and the main debate lies in how much has to be taken in order to have a positive effect on illness. During a cold or infection, the need for vitamin C can rocket, as it does during stress and exposure to pollution. Humans, apes, guinea pigs, and some species of fruit-eating bat are unable to make their own vitamin C. Humans have all the requirements for the synthesis of this vitamin except for the final liver enzyme, and must rely on dietary sources. Goats subjected to stress may manufacture thousands of milligrams of vitamin C in order to cope with it, and a number of researchers think that in order to fight an infection some people may need up to 10 grams, or more, of this nutrient for a number of days.

Vitamin C seems to enhance the movement of scavenger cells and increase the production of T-lymphocytes and antibodies. It is a very important weapon against free-radicals, unstable compounds which can damage cell walls and make it easier for bacteria, toxins and viruses to invade the body. Vitamin C has antihistamine qualities and can help to dry nasal secretions. It can also strengthen white blood cells by activating the body's protective protein, interferon. Vitamin C can be deadly to all types of viruses; it is important for the body's recuperative powers, and is involved in the elimination of toxins. Bioflavonoids work with vitamin C, increasing its effectiveness and retention.

Daily doses of over 500mg a day of vitamin C should be avoided by anyone taking the contraceptive pill, as more than this can have the effect of changing a low-dose oestrogen containing pill to a high-dose pill, therefore increasing the risk of some side-effects. See Chapter 9 for other important information about vitamin C's interaction with medicines. Daily doses of over 1000mg of vitamin C can increase breast tenderness in some women. People suffering from gastric ulcers should only take vitamin C as calcium ascorbate, to prevent stomach irritation, and anyone who has hyperoxaluria should consult their doctor before taking large supplemental doses of this nutrient. During pregnancy, avoid taking more than 500mg of vitamin C per day. Anyone taking large doses of vitamin C should also take calcium, magnesium, and B12 in supplemental form.

- **Vitamin E** enhances antibody response in conjunction with EPA — the oil found in fatty fish, and carotene — the form of vitamin A found in vegetables and fruit. Selenium and vitamin E together enhance lymphocyte activity and the production of antibodies.

- **Zinc** is important for moving vitamin A reserves to the tissues. It is involved in the production of T-lymphocytes and is vital for the thymus gland where these cells mature. In tandem with iron, zinc is important for activating the immune system; it also works with vitamin C to power the white blood cells, and its effectiveness is enhanced in conjunction with vitamins A and B6, and with the mineral phosphorus.

IMMUNE NUTRIENTS QUICK REFERENCE CHART

The foods in this chart are listed in alphabetical rather than descending order. This is because where and how foods are grown and stored can make quite a difference to their nutritional content; however, those marked with a star (*) usually contain highter amounts of the specific vitamins or minerals listed.

For details of the effects on requirements of medicines, see Chapter 9.

Nutrient	Significant food sources	Requirements increased by
Vitamin A Pre-formed	Cheese*, egg yolk, fish liver oils*, liver*, whole milk.	Cold weather, diabetes, liver disease, strenuous physical activity, mineral oil, cortisone, insufficient vitamin D, high intake of alcohol, coffee, food preservatives, fried foods and iron.
Pro-formed	Broccoli*, carrots, mangoes*, olives, papaya (paw-paw), parsley*, pumpkin*, sunflower seeds, watercress.	
B-complex	Brewer's yeast*, egg yolk, liver* milk yogurt and cheese, most vegetables and fruit, nuts, peas and beans, rice bran*, seafoods, whole grains, wheatgerm.	Alcohol, oral contraceptives, coffee, infections, stress, excessive sugar intake, smoking, medicines.

Nutrient	Significant food sources	Requirements increased by
Vitamin B5	Brewer's yeast*, egg yolk, milk yogurt and cheese*, peas and beans, royal jelly*, wheatgerm, whole grains.	Stress, injury, allergies, medicines.
Vitamin B12	Brewer's yeast, cheese and yogurt*, kelp, miso and tempeh, organ meats*, sardines, spirulina (plant plankton)*.	Alcohol, B6 deficiency, coffee, calcium deficiency, iron deficiency, laxatives, liver disease, oral contraceptives, other medicines.†
Vitamin C	Blackberries, blackcurrants, Brussels sprouts citrus fruits, green peppers*, kale, papaya*, parsley, watercress*.	Fever, stress, smoking, strenuous activity, oral contraceptives, other medicines.

†Although seaweeds, miso, tempeh and spirulina do contain B12, recent research suggests that these sources may not be easily absorbed by the body. If you are a vegan or vegetarian who relies solely on these foods for your source of B12, it may be important for you to take a B12 supplement, or ask your doctor to give you occasional B12 injections, especially if you are breastfeeding a baby.

Nutrient	Significant food sources	Requirements increased by
Bioflavonoids	apricots buckwheat (green)* grapes lemon including the juice* papaya rosehips skin and pith of citrus fruit*	See vitamin C.
Vitamin D	Dairy products, egg yolk, herring, liver, mackerel, salmon, sardines.	Lack of exposure to sunlight, vegan diet, medicines, high intake of fried foods.
Vitamin E	Avocado, cold-pressed vegetable oils*, dark green leafy vegetables, egg yolk, sesame seeds and tahini, sunflower seeds/ butter, wheatgerm and wheatgerm oil*, whole grains.	Air pollution, oral contraceptives, chlorine in drinking water, high consumption of refined foods, strenuous activity, high intake of polyunsaturated fats or oils, infections, diabetes, medicines.

Nutrient	Significant food sources	Requirements increased by
Calcium	Brewer's yeast, carob, cheese and milk products*, nuts, seaweeds especially hijiki, sesame seeds and tahini*, wheatgerm, yogurt*.	Stress, excessive phosphorus and saturated fats, alcohol, infection, excessive perspiration and fever, medicines.
Folic acid	Beans and peas, brewer's yeast, eggs, fatty fish, green leafy vegetables, liver, nuts, soy flour, wheatgerm, wholegrains.	Alcohol, illness, injury, stress, smoking, oral contraceptives, other medicines.
Iron	Brewer's yeast, dried fruit*, egg yolk*, green leafy vegetables*, liver and other lean meats*, molasses*, parsley, water-cress, wheatgerm.	Coffee, tea, excessive copper or zinc, heavy bleeding, strenuous physical activity, medicines.

Nutrient	Significant food sources	Requirements increased by
Magnesium	Apples, avocado, bananas, bean, peas and lentils, black grapes and raisins, brewer's yeast, fish and seafoods, green leafy vegetables, most nuts and seeds, soya flour, wheatgerm, whole grains.	Abnormally high or low protein intake, burns, diarrhoea, heavy perspiration or fever, high intake of coffee or tea, alcohol, high intake of sugar or refined foods, stress, shock, surgery, medicines.
Selenium	Asparagus, brewer's yeast, eggs, fish, garlic* and onions, organ meats, whole grains.	Diet high in processed and refined foods, environmental pollution, lipid-lowering drugs.
Zinc	Brewer's yeast, brown rice, eggs and dairy products, herring, liver and other organ meats, most vegetables,	Oral contraceptives, diabetes, diet high in refined or processed foods, excessive perspiration or fever, high carbohydrate, low protein intake, alcohol, medicines.

Nutrient	Significant food sources	Requirements increased by
Zinc (cont.)	pumpkin seeds, seafood, wheatgerm, whole grain yeast risen breads.	

SUPPLEMENTARY STRATEGIES

The nutritional value of the food you eat depends very much upon where and how it was grown. Some of the fresh produce we eat in the winter is imported, and this results in the loss of a percentage of vitamins during transport and storage. Because of this, it may sometimes be necessary to take preventive supplemental action, and this section will help you to get the balance right. It is better, where possible, to get the nutrition you need from food rather than tablets, but during the winter it is often important to supplement the diet. Vitamin C, which is vital for the immune system, is greatly depleted by transport and storage.

An imported orange, far from bursting with vitamin C, is likely to contain less than 5mg by the time you eat it. Smoking or exposure to others' smoke, stress, infection, illness, and some medicines escalate requirements of this vitamin.

The following suggestions can help you to choose the right supplements for a healthier winter, but if you would like individual dietary help from an alternative/complementary practitioner see Finding a Natural Practitioner in Chapter 11.

CHILDREN

By the time children reach school-age it may be necessary to include some form of supplementation in their diet, to help the body cope with growth and new stresses, especially during the winter. The immune system is usually quite vigorous and may only need a gentle nudge to help it function well, but exposure to chemicals in the school environment can weaken its response. This is also the time when you begin to have less control over what a child eats during the day. Foods with high nutrient levels can be given to 'supplement' the diet, and these include rice bran, fresh wheat germ, ground sesame or sunflower seed meal, a very small quantity of kelp powder, and cod liver oil. These can all be added to foods, and their presence need not be obvious. *Bio Strath*, *Kindervital*, and *Floradix* are all natural liquid supplements made from yeast, herbs, fruit and vegetables, and, taken daily with a wholefood diet and concentrated food sources, will provide the basis for excellent nutrition, and improve winter health. If vitamin C intake needs to be increased, then rosehip tea added to fresh fruit juice can provide extra, or perhaps a little powdered vitamin C as calcium ascorbate can be added to the child's drink once or twice a day; however, the dose does not usually need to exceed 300mg.

Teenagers need optimum nutrition, and the same dietary suggestions as for young children should be followed, with the addition of a multiple vitamin/mineral tablet that supplies at least 25mg of B complex vitamins and 500mg of vitamin C. This may be taken once or twice a day with a meal.

ADULTS

A well-balanced wholefood diet is the basis for good winter health but it is sometimes necessary to include more concentrated sources of nutrients in the diet, especially during periods of prolonged stress, illness, cold weather or dieting, if you are a smoker, or at times when alcohol is consumed or prescription medicines are taken. To find out whether you are taking a medicine that may be depleting your nutritional status, see Chapter 9.

Follow the general dietary guidelines in this chapter, and if necessary take a daily multiple vitamin/mineral tablet. If separate supplements can be afforded, the following chart will provide a general guide to follow when choosing what to take this winter.

Supplement	B'fast	Lunch	Supper	Bedtime
Vit. C 500mg	1	1	1	
Vit. A 2,500iu	1			
B-complex 50mg	1	1		
Vit. E 400iu*	1			
Zinc 30mg				1
Calcium 1000mg				1
Magnesium 500mg				1
Selenium 100mcg	1			
Royal Jelly	1			

* Before taking supplements check Chapter 9 to see whether any medicines you may be taking will interact. If you suffer from rheumatic heart disease, or are taking digitalis, beta blockers or other heart medicines, then vitamin E should only be taken in supplement form under your doctor's guidance. If you have mitral stenosis, then taking vitamin E in doses greater than 30iu per day may increase the incidence of chest pains. If you are susceptible to very high blood pressure, vitamin E should be started at a dose no greater than 100iu a day and gradually increased; this should be done with your doctor's advice. If you have breast cancer, seek your doctor's advice before taking vitamin E, and if you are an insulin-dependent diabetic, consult a doctor before taking supplemental vitamin E as the insulin dose may need to be adjusted in accordance with the amount of vitamin E to be used.

ADULTS OVER 65

Follow the general dietary guidelines in this chapter, and it can also be helpful for you to include a daily vitamin and mineral supplement, especially if your are taking medicines every day. Multi-vites are relatively inexpensive, but should provide up to 500mg of vitamin C, and up to 30mg of zinc. It is preferable to use a liquid or soft capsule vitamin and mineral formula as this will be absorbed and utilized more easily. If the budget allows for separate supplements to be purchased, then a recommended daily regime could include the following.

Supplement	B'fast	Lunch	Supper	Bedtime
Vit. C 250mg	1		1	
Vit. A 2,500iu	1			
B-complex 25mg	1	1		
Vit. E 200iu*	1			
Zinc 30mg				1
Calcium 1000mg				1
Magnesium 500mg				1
Selenium 100mcg	1			
Royal Jelly	1			

* See the warning about vitamin E supplements in the previous section. If your doctor is willing to give you regular B12 injections it may help you to weather the winter better and improve your general feeling of well-being.

IMMUNE-BOOSTING AND WARMING DRINKS

Food or beverages do not need to be hot to help you create body heat, because the body uses the components of food — protein, carbohydrates, and fats — to make heat. A hot drink will actually make you lose a little body heat by dilating the blood vessels, but the warmth you take in with the liquid will counterbalance this effect. Holding a mug of warm soup or a hot drink warms the hands and provides a feeling of comforting warmth, but a large quantity of liquid would need to be consumed at 130°F to create any *extra* body heat.

The following ideas include both warm and cool drinks. They are especially suitable for school-age children as an alternative to colas and fizzy drinks, and provide a good-tasting and easily digested nutritional boost.

Hot Stuff
1 pint organic apple juice
1 unpeeled organic orange, sliced
½ teaspoon cinnamon
pinch nutmeg
3 cloves

Place the ingredients in a covered non-aluminium saucepan and bring slowly to a light boil. If you use an electric hotplate, allow to simmer over a low heat for 5 minutes, then turn the hotplate off and allow the residual heat to keep it simmering for another 4–5 minutes. If using gas, turn the flame down, and allow to simmer for 5–10 minutes, then strain. Enjoy while hot, and add a squeeze of fresh lemon juice. This recipe will make enough for four cups.

Calcium Cocktail
Increase your calcium and protein intake with this tasty, quickly prepared drink.

1 tablespoon freshly ground sesame seeds, or 1 tablespoon tahini
6–8 oz plain 'live' yogurt
1 teaspoon brewer's yeast flakes
1 tablespoon carob powder
1 large, ripe banana
½ teaspoon bee pollen granules
1 teaspoon fresh wheatgerm

Put the ingredients into a blender and mix until creamy smooth. Drink slowly, and mix well with the saliva in your mouth to ensure good digestion.

Carob Chill-Chaser

If chocolate is off your food list, here is a substitute that does not contain refined sugar, caffeine or high levels of fat. A mug of hot carob milk warms you up and supplies plenty of minerals especially calcium.

1 pint unsweetened milk of your choice
1 tablespoon carob powder
Small piece of vanilla pod to taste
Date syrup or honey to taste

In a non-aluminium saucepan, use a wooden spoon to mix the carob powder and a little milk into a paste. If you require a sweetener, add a little honey or date syrup at this point, then slowly pour in the remainder of the milk and stir until blended. Add a small piece of vanilla pod and slowly heat the drink, but do not allow it to come to a boil. Enough for two large mugfuls.

Ginger and Mint Zinger

Both ginger and mint are warming herbs and, in combination with cinnamon and cloves, will give you a warm glow all over.

2 teaspoons freshly grated ginger root
2 teaspoons honey, or more, to taste
1 large cinnamon stick, broken into thirds
6 cloves
1 peppermint teabag
1 pint filtered or mineral water

Put all the ingredients except the peppermint teabag into a non-aluminium saucepan, put the lid on and bring to the boil. Lower the heat and simmer for 30 minutes. Turn off the heat and add the peppermint teabag. Allow to steep for 3 minutes, then strain and pour while hot. This recipe will make four cups.

Protein-Packed Zinc Drink

It takes five minutes to prepare this protein- and nutrient-packed drink, but it can help your body create warmth for hours.

4 oz milk or soya milk
2 oz pineapple chunks in natural juice
1 tablespoon lecithin granules
2 teaspoons freshly ground sesame seeds
or 1 tablespoon tahini
¼ teaspoon grated raw ginger
2 tablespoons freshly ground pumpkin seeds
1-2 teaspoons sugar-free jam, or a peeled banana
¼ teaspoon natural vanilla extract

Put the ingredients into a blender and mix well. Sip slowly, and mix with the saliva in your mouth by 'chewing' it well before swallowing: this will aid digestion.

Winter Warmer

A welcome warming drink for cold winter evenings. To make two cups, gently heat the following ingredients in a saucepan:

16 oz unsweetened blackcurrant, cherry, or raspberry juice
1 teaspoon freshly grated ginger
1 cinnamon stick, or ¼ teaspoon cinnamon powder
¼ teaspoon aniseed
¼ teaspoon fennel seeds
1 chamomile teabag

Put all the ingredients except the chamomile teabag into a non-aluminium saucepan. Bring to the boil, reduce the heat and simmer for 10 minutes. Turn off the heat, add the chamomile teabag, and then allow to steep for 5 minutes, strain, and sip slowly.

GROWING FRESH FOOD IN THE WINTER

During the winter much of our fresh food is imported, or grown in greenhouses. Often the foods are subjected to a battery of chemicals, or are nutritionally limp by the time they reach the table. If you enjoy growing vegetables, it is possible to plan your garden so that there will be a supply of fresh winter vegetables including Brussels sprouts, cabbage, leeks, cauliflower, and sprouting broccoli. Carrots can be harvested in the winter by growing them during the summer months, and leaving them in the ground, safe from the frost, covered with a thick insulating layer of hay. For more information about growing fresh vegetables in the winter, see *Food From Your Garden* by Brian Walkden (Thorsons 1979).

INDOOR GARDENING

With a little patience it is possible to produce inexpensive, organically grown plants which can add fresh nutritional value to winter meals.

Wheatgrass Crop

Wheatgrass juice is a powerhouse of vitamins, minerals, chlorophyll and enzymes, all of which are vital to health, especially during the winter. To produce a fresh crop of wheatgrass you will need:

2–4 old ceramic baking dishes or glass roasting trays
fertile garden soil or organic potting compost
a small bag of organically grown whole wheat grains
a small watering can fitted with a rose.

Soak the grains overnight in lukewarm filtered water before sowing. Save the water they were soaked in to use when sowing. Place the earth in the containers so that it almost reaches the rim. Sprinkle the wheat grains liberally over the soil, water them in, then cover with wet newspaper, avoiding coloured newsprint which contains lead. Place a plastic bag over the tray to keep in the warmth and moisture. As the sprouts begin pushing up the covers, remove them and place the tray in a warm, sunny window.

Wheatgrass can be harvested when it reaches about 6–7 inches (15–18cm). At this point it has a sweet flavour, similar to aniseed. Grasp a handful of the grass, and cut it about half an inch from the roots. When the wheatgrass has reached the point of harvest for the second time it should be re-seeded: pull it up gently by the roots, and start again.

Fresh wheatgrass juice can be made by running it, and well-washed roots, through a meat grinder, catching the juice in a glass jug with a strainer over the mouth. If you own an electric juicer, the juice from the grass and roots can be extracted with the machine. A tray of mature wheatgrass may be stored in a refrigerator for up to five days.

Fresh Dandelion Leaves

Dandelions are a rich source of vitamin A, iron, and other nutrients vital for the immune system. They have very long roots, so an old fish tank is an ideal indoor garden for them. Because dandelions are hardy, they will be perfectly content to grow in plain garden soil. Place small stones or pebbles in the bottom of the tank to a depth of about 2 inches (5 cm), and then add some earth from your garden until the tank is about half full.

To get a head start on growing dandelions, take a trowel into your garden and dig up some good specimens in mid-September. Dig a circle, at least 3–4 inches (8–10 cm) round the plant, and approximately 8 inches (20cm) deep, lift the plant and earth out carefully so as not to damage the roots. Transfer the dandelion and earth to the tank, leaving about 3 inches (8 cm) between plants. Add more soil to the tank so that the gaps between the plants are filled. A medium-sized tank should accommodate about six plants. Water them well in with filtered tap water, using a rose on the watering can, then keep them moist by watering about every two days.

When grown indoors, dandelions will keep producing new leaves, and once a week it will be possible to pick one or two outer leaves from each plant and add them to salads. Wash them well, and if mould forms on the leaves discard them. If the plants die, they need not be wasted as the roots can be washed and roasted in the oven to make dandelion coffee. The roots have diuretic properties, and are considered to be healthy for the liver.

Simple-To-Grow Sprouts

Sprouts are easy to grow and provide valuable vitamin C. They are a fresh, organically-grown addition to winter salads. Sprouting is very inexpensive and the only equipment needed is a large glass jar, a piece of clean cheesecloth, and a rubber band. Organically grown seeds and pulses can be obtained from wholefood stores, and those which make pleasant tasting sprouts include alfalfa, mung beans, radish, lentils, fenugreek, and aduki beans. Alfalfa seeds will sprout within 2–4 days and the beans may take from 4–8 days.

Place about ¾ inch (2cm) of seeds in the bottom of a large glass jar, then transfer them to a sieve and rinse them well. Put them back in the jar and place cheesecloth over the mouth, securing it with a rubber band. Rinse the seeds once more, and drain the water out through the cloth. Place the container in a dark cupboard overnight, away from cleaning chemicals. The seeds/beans should then be rinsed and drained three times a day with filtered spring water. Leave them in a sunny window. Alfalfa is ready when its sprouts are about ¾ inch long with tiny green leaves at the top. Lentils are edible when their sprout has reached about ¼ inch, and spicy radish sprouts are ready to eat when they turn pink/red and measure approximately ½–¾ inch. Beans vary, but the sprout may be anything from ½–1 inch long when they are ready to eat.

Use sprouts in salads, on sandwiches, or in cooked dishes. Start another jar of sprouts about three days after the first, so that there will be a continuing supply of fresh sprouts. Grow different sprouts each time to provide variety. The sprouts can be stored in the fridge up to five days. If the sprouts smell, or taste, mouldy or acidic DO NOT eat them, but throw them away, wash the jar and cloth extremely well, and start again.

Mustard and Cress

Mustard and cress seeds are obtainable from hardware stores and garden centres, and can easily be grown in a sunny window. Sow the cress quite thickly on a piece of damp matting in a plate or tray, place one end of the matting in a shallow container of water to keep it moist. Three days later sow the mustard, and the crop should be ready within about three more days. Make sure that the temperature does not drop below 45°F. Keep the cycle going with two crops by sowing the second batch about three days after the first one. If the sprouts smell mouldy or acidic, do not eat them.

More Ideas

For more ideas about indoor gardening, check Thorsons' line of gardening and 'self-sufficient living' books. If you have installed full spectrum lighting (see Chapters 6 and 11) in your home, both you and your indoor garden will benefit.

WINTER STORE CUPBOARD

Stock an emergency cupboard by purchasing one or two items during shopping trips in the autumn, in case bad weather or illness prevents you from going out. Choose foods which are free from additives, preservatives, colourings and lots of E numbers. Buy store brands if they are cheaper, and watch out for bargains, but never buy dented cans, and avoid keeping them for longer than two years. Fish, canned in oil, will last up to five years, as will solid-packed cold meats.

Keep the foods in your store cupboard fresh by occasionally using and replacing them. Check expiry dates regularly to ensure that the foods are not wasted. You may have some potatoes, eggs, vegetables, onions, fruit, milk, or other items in the house, and these can be used in conjunction with the stored items to provide more variety. Keep some fresh ginger root in your refrigerator, and this can be grated into cooking for its warming value.

USEFUL ITEMS

A variety of dried or canned lentils and beans
2 or 3 cans of fruit in natural juice
A variety of canned vegetables without additives or excessive salt or sugar
(if you have no freezer)
2–3 cans of preservative- and additive-free soups
2–3 packs of natural fruit with added vitamin C
1 tin each of tuna, sardines, and salmon
A variety of dried fruit
Wholegrain cereal
Well-sealed pack of porridge oats
Brown rice
Soya milk or dried, skimmed milk
Vegetable stock cubes

FREEZER ITEMS

Variety of frozen vegetables
Frozen goat milk (freezes well and will remain for up to three months)
A couple of your favourite loaves of wholemeal bread
Meat
Fish
One or two quick-to-prepare natural frozen meals

WHAT TO EAT DURING A POWER CUT

If your electricity fails and you cook with electricity, try to avoid eating lots of sugary snacks such as biscuits or cake. Remember that you do not have to eat hot foods in order for your body to create warmth. If you are unable to cook, then you can still provide your body with the nutrients it uses to stay warm. Try making simple sandwiches with salmon, tuna, or sardines, or enjoy some milk and wholegrain cereal, or canned fruit with soy milk.

BIBLIOGRAPHY

Marvin Sahud & Richard J. Cohen, 'Aspirin and Platelet Count, and Vitamin C', Lancet, 8 May 1971.

S. Ananda, et al., 'Serum Thymulin and Zinc Deficiency in Humans', American Journal of Clinical Nutrition 45, 4, p. 873, April 1987.

'Zinc and the Thymus', Lancet, 5 May 1984.

'Single Nutrient Effects on Immunology Functions', Journal of The American Medical Association 245, pp. 53–58, 2 January 1981.

'Evidence of Factors Associated With the Depression of Immunity in Malnutrition', American Journal of Clinical Nutrition 27: pp. 665–669, 1974.

'Intestinal Bacteria and Their Role in Infection', Lancet 2, pp. 724–727, 1968.

M. Bunk, et al., 'Dietary Zinc Deficiency and Vitamin E Transport', American Journal of Clinical Nutrition, 45:865, 1987.

D. VanderJagt, et al., 'Ascorbic Acid Intake and Plasma Levels in Healthy

74

Elderly People', *American Journal of Clinical Nutrition*, 46, pp 290–4, 1987.

C. Pinnoc, et al., 'Vitamin A Status in Children who are Prone to Respiratory Tract Infections', Australian Paediatric In. 22, 2, pp. 95–99, May 1986.

A. Bradley, A. Theobold, 'Are We Obtaining Adequate Vitamins and Minerals From our Diet', *Journal of Human Nutrition and Diet* 1, 105, 1988.

A.J. Thomas, et al., 'Inpatients Deficient in Essential Nutrients' *British Journal of Nutrition* 59, 181, 1988.

N.W. Solomons, R.M. Russell, 'The Interaction of Vitamin A and Zinc: Implications for Human Nutrition', *American Journal of Clinical Nutrition* 33, pp. 2031–40, 1980.

J.C. Smith Jr, et al., 'Zinc a Trace Element Essential in Vitamin A Metabolism', *Science* 181, pp. 954–5, 1973.

S. Blaza, et al., 'Thermogenic Response to Temperature, Exercise, and Food Stimulation in Lean and Obese Women', *British Journal of Clinical Nutrition* 42, pp. 171–80, 1983.

Helen M.V. Newton B.Sc. et al., 'The Cause and Correction of Low Blood Vitamin C Concentrations in the Elderly', *American Journal of Clinical Nutrition* 42, 4, pp. 656–59, Oct. 1985.

L. Hoffman-Goetz, M.J. Kluger, 'Protein Deficiency: its Effects on Body Temperature in Health and Disease States', *American Journal of Clinical Nutrition* 32, pp. 1423–7, 1979.

R.G. Smith, M.B., Ch.B., F.R.C.P.E., 'Zinc May be Important in the Elderly Patient's Ability to Resist Infection', *Geriatric Medicine* 17, 7, p. 18 July 1987.

L.V. Avioli, 'Absorption and Metabolism of Vitamin D3 in Man', *American Journal of Clinical Nutrition* 22, pp. 437–45, 1969.

M.J. Kluger, et al., 'Fever and Survival', *Science* 188, pp. 166–8, 1975.

M.J. Kluger, et al., 'Fever and Reduced Iron: Their Interaction as a Host Defense Response', *Science* 203, pp. 374–6, 1979.

M.J. Murray, A.B. Marray, 'Anorexia of Infection as a Mechanism of Host Defense, *American Journal of Clinical Nutrition* 32, pp. 593–6, 1979.

J. MacHauglin, M.F. Holick, 'Ageing Decreases the Capacity of Human

Skin to Produce vitamin D3', *Journal of Clinical Investigation* 76, pp. 1536–8, 1985.

L.E. Skinner, M.R. Willis, 'Seasonal Variations in Serum 25-Hydroxyvitamin D in the Elderly in Britain', *Lancet* 1, pp. 979–80, 1979.

D.E.M. Lawson, et al., 'Relative Contributions of Diet and Sunlight to Vitamin D State in the Elderly', *British Medical Journal* 2, pp. 303–5, 1979.

H.M. Hodkinson, et al., 'Sunlight, Vitamin D and Ostomalacia in the Elderly', *Lancet* 1, pp. 910–12, 1973.

C. Lamberg-Allardt, 'Vitamin D Intake, Sunlight Exposure and 25-Hydroxyvitamin D Levels in the Elderly During One Year, *Annals of Nutritional Metabolism* 28, pp. 144–50, 1984.

M. Taylor-Baer, Ph.D., et al., 'Nitrogen Utilization, Enzyme Activity, Glucose Intolerance, and Leukocyte Chemotaxis in Human Experimental Zinc Depletion', *American Journal of Clinical Nutrition* 41, pp. 1220–1235, June 1986.

K.M. Hambridge, 'Zinc and Chromium in Human Nutrition, *Journal of Human Nutrition* 32, pp. 99-110, 1987.

R.S. Pekarek, et al., 'Abnormal Cellular Immune Responses During Acquired Zinc Deficiency', *American Journal of Clinical Nutrition* 32, pp. 1253–9, 1979.

M. Brook, J.J. Grimshaw, 'Vitamin C Concentrations of Plasma and Leukocytes as Related to Smoking Habits, Age, and Sex of Humans', *American Journal of Clinical Nutrition* 21, pp. 1254–8, 1968.

Gillian Martlew ND and Shelley Silver, *The Medicine Chest*, Thorsons, 1988.

Gillian Martlew ND and Shelley Silver, *The Pill Protection Plan*, Thorsons, 1989.

J. Bernestine et al., 'Depression of Lymphocyte Transformation Following Oral Glucose Ingestion', *American Journal of Clinical Nutrition* 30, p. 613, 1977.

A. Sanchez, et al., 'Role of Sugar in Human Neutrophic Phagocytosis', *American Journal of Clinical Nutrition* 26, pp. 1180–84, 1973.

Chapter 4

INDOORS — POLLUTION AND SOLUTIONS

'The very first canon of nursing is to keep the air inside as fresh as the air outside, by night as well as by day.'

Florence Nightingale

TO BREATHE, OR NOT TO BREATHE . . .

Many ancient civilizations believed in the curative powers of fresh air and sunlight, but by medieval times, especially in western culture, the idea had been lost, and even reversed. By the seventeenth century the medical establishment was doing its best to convince everyone that fresh air was a hazard. The rich slept in four-poster beds protected from the cold and miasmas in the 'evil' night air by thick bed curtains and night-caps, and the sick were sealed in stifling rooms, a practice which was probably responsible for hastening their departure from this world. These ideas survived into the Victorian era, and nineteenth century furniture and drapery often decreased the amount of sunlight and air entering rooms.

AIR QUALITY

It is only comparatively recently in our history that we have shut ourselves away from the elements, and as a result our exposure to fresh air has been diminishing. It has now reached the point where up to 90 per cent of us spend at least 75 per cent of our time in buildings or vehicles.

Because of the way the body takes in air, we are vulnerable to air pollution and air-borne contaminants. Every breath we take passes from the thin cell walls of thousands of alveoli — airbag-like structures in the lungs — out into the bloodstream, where the oxygen and other gases are carried around the whole body. By breathing through the nose rather than the mouth, we can ensure that some of the pollutants we are exposed to are filtered out. The inside of the nostrils and the bronchial tubes in the lungs are covered with tiny 'hairs' called cilia which, due to their wave-like motion, transport dust, dirt, and other impurities out of the airways. The nose traps bacteria in the mucus manufactured by its mucous membranes, and it also warms and moistens the air before it reaches our lungs.

Oxygen is so vital to us that if the brain is deprived of this element for only ten seconds, the result may be a coma. Oxygen starvation for three minutes or more may result in permanent damage to the brain. It is not just the brain that requires a constant supply of oxygen; all the cells in the body need it to produce energy, and even a slight drop in the oxygen available to us can result in feelings of lethargy.

The air we breathe should be the breath of life, but sometimes our lifestyle, the homes we live in, and many of the things we surround ourselves with have the potential to change air from a life-giver to a source of ill-health, and because we are not always able to see or smell air-borne contaminants, we may not be aware that the air surrounding us is adversely affecting the way we feel.

INDOOR CHEMICAL EXPOSURE

Staying indoors for long periods of time can make some people feel ill. During the winter we tend to spend a great proportion of the day sealed against the weather in houses and offices where the air may be heated, polluted, and stale. It is quite common to hear complaints about tiredness, headaches, dry skin, stuffy nose, listlessness, irritability, frequent infections, and even nausea, when people are confined to closed buildings for long periods of time. There are several reasons for this: the quality of light and air are major factors, and although it is well-known that a reduced level of oxygen can cause tiredness and fatigue, there are other air quality problems which may not be so readily apparent; air pollution, and an increase in positively charged air ions can quite dramatically affect the way we feel.

Few of us see our warm homes as having the potential to undermine health but in fact the possibility is even greater than we realize — we live in an age of synthetic materials, which may not be as inert as we like to think. As our lifestyles have become more sophisticated, so too, have the things we share our homes with. Unlike our ancestors, we no longer have to contend with heating and cooking methods which fill houses with choking smoke, but the new age has brought with it more insidious and less obvious health hazards.

The problem of indoor pollution increases as we close ourselves more tightly into our homes in the winter, and introduce more chemically manufactured substances into the environment. Our desire for draught-free homes has produced a whole new generation of health problems. Double glazing and draft excluders make houses warmer but they also reduce the amount of fresh air entering the building. Draughty windows and a lit fire ensure a flow of air into the room because the fire pulls air from between ill-fitting window frames and sucks it, and combustion chemicals, up the chimney. On the other hand, closed fires and central heating do not encourage a flow of fresh air into the building. Draught-proofing, if combined with inadequate ventilation, seals us in an environment filled with potential health dangers. When fresh air is reduced, pollutants can build up to levels where they undermine our health. Numerous problems including headaches, migraine, allergies, and breathing disorders can all be linked with indoor pollution.

Gas and oil appliances need to be located where there is adequate ventilation because combustion chemicals constantly leak into the air. Gas fires require adequate ventilation, to enhance their burning efficiency and to dilute waste gases. Gas appliances produce harmful combustion by-products including formaldehyde, sulphur dioxide, hydrogen cyanide, nitric acid, carbon monoxide, and nitrogen oxide. The same is true of fireplaces and woodstoves which produce a number of dangerous combustion chemicals.

CHEMICALS AND POLLUTANTS IN DISGUISE

Smoking is a well-known source of indoor air pollution, but apparently innocuous appliances like gas cookers or even old books and talcum powder are potential polluters. Other seemingly harmless objects can undermine health. For instance, chipboard, hardboard, carpets, new clothes, furniture, plywood, and fibreglass insulation all appear to be inert, but they are often significant sources of indoor pollution because they may contain formaldehyde. This pungent gas is used as a disinfectant, bonding material, and preservative, and is also found in fabric treatments. Formaldehyde seeps into the air from products containing it. In buildings and homes this may be the root of a number of health problems from irritability to headaches and nausea.

Plastics are fast becoming one of the most common substances in homes, the work-place and vehicles. Plastics are made from coal and petroleum and are capable of a phenomenon called 'outgassing' which is the slow but continuous release of their chemical constituents into the air. We are not generally aware of this until entering a car which as been standing in the hot sun. Plastics emit vapours, especially when heated, and in a hot, confined space the smell of plasticizers becomes extremely noticeable. For people who are sensitive, this may produce an almost instant feeling of nausea or it may cause headaches.

Pollutants even exist in the bathroom. If you close yourself in the room for a morning shower, dust yourself liberally with talcum, and use a spray deodorant and hairspray, then you will have begun your day with exposure to a cocktail of four different types of indoor pollution.

Scientists studying the effect of breathing the moist air in and around showers have suggested that taking a long, hot shower exposes you to trichlorethylene chloroform, a by-product of chlorine which is found in the water vapour. To reduce your exposure, use cooler water, limit the shower to no more than five minutes and open the bathroom window. Talcum powder is similar to asbestos, and numerous studies have linked it with a serious form of lung damage called talcosis. Once inhaled, the talcum is not cleared from the lungs, and causes damage because it remains in the delicate lung tissue. Cornflour is a safe, inexpensive alternative; it will not make you smell exotic, but it does have the advantage of being safer. If you use a spray deodorant, consider switching to a roll-on for your own and for the environment's sake. The danger of using hairspray can be reduced by switching to a pump-action spray, ensuring there is adequate ventilation in the room, and holding your breath while actually spraying hair. Open a window and leave the room immediately after using the product.

Many mass-market cosmetics, soaps, perfumes, and detergents are petroleum based, and a large percentage of the population is allergic to these without being aware of it. A trip to the Body Shop will provide safe alternatives to many of these chemical-based products, and may cure the irritable, headachy feelings which occur every morning in some households.

See Dietary Defence at the end of this chapter for information about protecting the body against pollutants.

CLEANER ALTERNATIVES

Many food, drink, and drug products are suspected of being detrimental to health because of the chemicals and additives they contain. More and more people are consuming products with fewer chemical additives because they are concerned about the effects of these on health. However, most shopping trips still include the purchase of a large variety of chemicals — disguised as household cleaners, aerosols, and solvents. Many of these products have a great potential for adversely affecting health, and yet it is very rare to find a health warning or even a list of ingredients on most packages.

The familiar conglomerations of cans and tubs under most sinks are not an obvious source of pollution, and they are rarely considered as pollutants when not in use.

Chemicals can, and do, migrate into the air from bottles and sprays, even when they are inactive, and for sensitive individuals these can be a major source of ill-health.

For the rest of us, these pollutants can prey on our health in a more deceptive way, and no one really seems to know what the combination of these chemicals, when used or stored together in a badly ventilated area, can have on health.

As worrying as all this may sound, there are steps we can take to protect ourselves from hidden environmental pollutants. Some are as simple as increasing ventilation or using more natural household products. Others can be tackled through the diet; see Dietary Defence in this chapter.

There are simple alternatives to the chemicals we have come to consider as essential for household cleanliness. Many of our grandparents can probably remember when the shops sold simple flakes of soap for cleaning clothes and floors, beeswax for polishing furniture, and sticky paper for catching flies. Now there is an overwhelming variety of brightly packaged products which promise to make life easier, surroundings more pleasant smelling, and germs run away screaming. Although many of these products do undoubtedly reduce the effort required to keep a home clean, they often do so at the expense of our health and the environment. Before reaching for a can of chemical cleaner, try a less harmful alternative from the list which follows.

Product	Natural alternative
Air freshener	Baking soda is an inexpensive but effective room and refrigerator deodorant. Instead of bathroom deodorizing sprays, strike a match; the sulphur kills unpleasant smells quickly and is less dangerous than aerosols. Keep the matches out of the reach of children.
	Another alternative is to keep a pot pourri in the room. In centrally heated rooms, put a few eucalyptus leaves into the water in simple radiator mounted humidifiers.
	Sprinkle baking soda into the bottom of dust bins and kitchen waste bins to decrease smells.

Product	Natural alternative
Disinfectant	Borax in hot water works as a disinfectant. The Ecover line of biodegradable products includes a toilet cleaner, see Chapter 11 for more details.
Mould cleaner	Try using baking soda and a stiff brush. Borax dissolved in warm water also removes mould.
Drain cleaner	For a drain blockage try using 4oz (110g) of baking soda and 8oz (220g) of vinegar in boiling water. Pour down the sink and leave overnight. Rinse well with hot water in the morning.
Furniture polish	There are natural beeswax polishes available at some health and hardware stores. A little more effort is required to produce a shine, but it is less likely than aerosol polishes to affect health.
Metal cleaner	A mixture of salt and lemon juice or vinegar can clean copper and bronze. For brass, a cleaner can be made by mixing together 1 tablespoon of salt, 2 tablespoons of flour and enough vinegar to make it into a paste. Cover the object with the paste, and when it is dry, wash it off with warm water and buff with a soft cloth.
Mould cleaner	Try using baking soda and a stuff brush. Borax dissolved in warm water also removes mould.
Oven cleaner	Make a paste from baking soda and water. Spread over the greasy area which needs

Product	Natural alternative
	cleaning and leave for about three minutes, then wash off with a scouring cloth and hot water — but never use an abrasive cloth on glass oven parts as it can cause them to shatter. As a preventative oven cleaner, sprinkle some salt on a spill immediately and simply brush it off when it cools. Chemical oven cleaners are one of the worst home-polluters, and despite extreme thoroughness of rinsing some of the chemicals remain in joints and corners; this residue will release fumes into the air again as soon as the oven is heated.
Rug cleaner	When a couple of inches of dry, powdery snow has fallen, take your small rugs outside and throw them face-down on it. This removes a large amount of dirt and more can be removed if the rug is beaten with a stick. The snow makes the rugs much brighter and they do not absorb very much moisture. When finished shake the rugs well and hang them for a few hours before replacing on the floor.
Tar and oil removal	To remove fresh tar and oil from clothes, fabric, and other items, soak a piece of cotton wool with eucalyptus oil and gently rub the soiled area. Allow the eucalyptus to soak into the fabric before washing it. Avoid using eucalyptus oil on perspex or plastic items, as it will melt them. The oil can be obtained from most chemists and some health stores.

Product	Natural alternative
Washing-up liquid	Ecover and Faith Products make biodegradable products that are kind to both the environment and your hands. See Chapter 11 for more information.
Window cleaner	Add about 1½ fl oz (40ml) of white vinegar to half a gallon (2 litres) of warm water. Transfer to a spray bottle to make window cleaning easier. To avoid 'fluff' on the windows, and make them sparkle, use a sheet of newspaper as a duster.

For more information on biodegradable cleaning and washing products, check Chapter 11.

OTHER ASPECTS OF AIR QUALITY

POSITIVE AND NEGATIVE IONS

The synthetic materials which surround us contribute to irritating gases in the home and they can also decrease the levels of healthy negative ions in the air. Predominantly positively- or negatively-charged air molecules can affect the way we feel. Confusingly, air which is over-charged with positive ions can have a negative effect on health, and air which is rich in negative ions can have a positive effect on health. (An ion is an air particle which carries an electrical charge; a negative ion is an atom or molecule which has gained an electron; and a positive ion is an atom or molecule which has lost an electron.)

The positive static charge produced by so many common objects in buildings reduces the level of negative ions. Metal articles and surfaces, electrical equipment, synthetic fabrics, and VDUs are all responsible for this phenomenon. Heating and air conditioning systems not only deplete the air of negative ions but also add positive ions to the air during recirculation. This is due to the creation of a positive charge as air passes across the metal. Electric bar fires and fan heaters are made with nickel chromium wire elements which generate positive ions when switched on.

Outside the home, high voltage equipment and power lines produce positive ions, and in nature positive ions are also created by radioactive emissions from soil and rocks, and by cosmic rays and hot dry winds. When there are high levels of positive ions in the air, scientists believe that the body responds by manufacturing too much of a powerful brain chemical, or neurotransmitter, known as serotonin. An excess of serotonin is thought to affect some of us by upsetting the nervous system and causing emotional and physical reactions such as fatigue, irritability, tension, anxiety, exhaustion, headaches, and breathing difficulties.

People who feel sleepy or relaxed after eating a large meal containing chicken or turkey may be reacting to slightly increased levels of this hormone, because these meats contain significant quantities of tryptophane, an amino acid which the body converts to serotonin. Levels of serotonin such as those produced by ingestion of tryptophane can induce natural relaxation and sleep.

Many families spend traditional winter holidays indoors with the heat and television on, and the windows shut. This is usually preceded by a substantial turkey dinner and very often there is a smoker in the room. All these factors add up to the production of excessive serotonin and there is a good chance that after a while drowsiness, lethargy and irritability will begin to creep up on some members of the family. The high levels of positive ions in the air, which increase serotonin, and the manufacture of more serotonin from tryptophane in the meat can induce these feelings.

Particles of dust are mostly positively charged and they carry micro-organisms such as bacteria and viruses into the body, via the lungs. Cigarette smoke contains a substantial variety of potential cancer-causing chemicals and it also attacks cilia, tiny 'hairs' which clear particles and foreign substances from the respiratory tract. Cilia line the nose, and bronchial tubes in the lungs, and move in a wave-like motion in order to carry pollutants out of the body. Smoke slows down the activity and effectiveness of the cilia, and so does stale air which contains a high proportion of positive ions.

The air inside a vehicle is often highly polluted and low in negative ions. As air passes over the metal body, or flows through air inlets, it becomes positively charged. This is one of the reasons why long-distance drivers feel tired and irritated, especially if the windows are closed and the heater is on.

THE POSITIVE EFFECTS OF NEGATIVE IONS

We have created internal environments that can make us feel ill, and although technology has contributed to this, it may also provide the answer.

It is possible to manufacture negative ions inside buildings and vehicles, with a special electrical unit called an ionizer. Placing an ionizer in a room or car restores the level of negative ions to stale and polluted, air because the negatively charged electrons attach to air gases such as oxygen and nitrogen.

Because the nervous system works by minute electrical impulses based on the principle of ion exchange, we can be sensitive to electrical alterations in the atmosphere. Extreme examples of this are the changes which take place before a storm. About a third of the world's population is thought to be sensitive to fluctuations in the air's electricity, especially the multiplication of positive ions which occurs with certain desert winds, or before a thunderstorm. Feelings of tiredness, sluggishness or headaches can build up until a storm breaks, and lightning, rain and wind create high levels of negative ions which counteract these feelings.

In nature negative ions are manufactured not just by the rain and lightning of storms, but also by sunshine, the movement of air, and the breaking up of water droplets in surf, rain, waterfalls, and fountains. Negative ions have a short lifespan and need to be manufactured constantly.

A high level of negative ions appears to increase the body's capacity to absorb oxygen, and decrease serotonin levels. This can reverse the unpleasant symptoms some people experience when inhaling stale and polluted air high in positive ions. Negative ions clean dust, smoke, airborne chemicals and metals from the air because the pollutants' positive charge attracts negative ions. When the particles become negatively charged they no longer float in the air but attach to surfaces near the ionizer, or fall to the floor where they will not be breathed in so easily.

Rebalancing the air's negative ions can offer some other benefits. People living or working with smokers, who find it uncomfortable to wear contact lenses because the smoke causes irritation, can try using an ionizer to solve the problem. Ionizers reduce the smoke in the air. Smokers and passive smokers can benefit too because negative ions help the body to eliminate smoke and airborne particles by increasing the beat of tiny 'hairs' which sweep pollutants out of the lungs.

Contact with other people in closed buildings, or vehicles, increases the chance of cross-infection. Using an ionizer may help to reduce airborne infections because bacteria travel in the air attached to dust particles. Negative ions precipitate the dust from the air, but they have also been shown to prevent bacteria from multiplying.

Because our living and working environments manufacture positive ions and destroy the healthy negative ions, changing some factors in our surroundings can help.

- ✔ If windows are opened periodically, stale indoor air is changed, and negative ions can enter the building.

- ✔ Try to avoid smoking or going into smoky atmospheres. Tobacco smoke can decrease the number of negative ions in the air.

- ✔ Avoid wearing synthetic clothing, and choose soft furnishings made from natural fabrics such as wool or cotton.

- ✔ Metal filing cabinets can be changed for wooden ones.

- ✔ Electrical equipment should be switched off when not in use.

A further solution is to install an ionizer. It will 'recondition' the air with negative ions even when the atmosphere outside is heavily charged with positive ions. For the majority of people this restores alertness and energy, and can offer a number of welcome health benefits as a result of decreased dust, smoke and pollution in the air.

DRY AIR

Humidity is a measure of the ratio of moisture in the air. We feel most comfortable when the air around us is humidified to about 35-50 per cent, but turning on the central heating can reduce the air's moisture by a quarter. Dry air is especially uncomfortable for people with asthma and other allergies because it causes feelings of stuffiness, dries air passages, and decreases the function of the cilia and respiratory tract mucus, thus increasing the chances of infection. When the air is very dry the skin suffers, and eyes become tired and irritated. To combat dry air in heated buildings, use a humidifier, preferably one with a humidistat that will monitor and control air moisture, because too much promotes the growth of house dust-mites, moulds and fungi. Ensure that the humidifier is cleaned regularly because the water reservoir is a favourite place for moulds, fungi, and algae to grow. These organisms will be ejected in the water aerosols and may be a cause of allergy for sensitive individuals. Use a solution of borax and hot water with a brush, and clean the machine at least once a week.

DUST AND DUST-MITES

Dust is composed of minute particles of earth, pollen, dead skin, fabrics, and other natural or synthetic substances. It is a household problem that has gradually increased since the introduction of soft furnishings and fitted carpets into the home. These items attract and hold dust, and their fabrics and fillings also contribute to the amount of dust in the environment. Walking across a carpet, sitting down in a chair, bouncing into bed, dusting with a dry cloth, vacuuming with most of the cleaners on the market, and making beds releases clouds of unseen dust and dust-mites into the air.

Dust is only obvious when it settles on furniture, but it can be seen clearly in a ray of sunlight or under a lamp. It is often surprising how much there is floating in the air, and although we give little thought to it, dust can affect our health. Dust dries air because it absorbs moisture, but it also transports micro-organisms into the lungs when they 'hitch a ride' on the particles in the air. Most people will react to a dusty environment by sneezing, but for some people dust can harbour the cause of severe asthma.

Common house dust itself does not seem to produce allergies; people are allergic to its tenants, the dust-mites. Dust-mites are microscopic parasites. They are present in our homes, and feast on the dead skin cells that are constantly sloughed off our bodies. They favour carpets, clothing, furniture, and especially beds, where the warm, moist conditions particularly appeal to them. Every time dust is stirred up, colonies of mites are propelled into the air, and breathed in. For anyone with asthma, the mites and their waste products are one of the largest single causes of suffocating asthma attacks.

Dust Busters

A percentage of house dust can be kept under control by regular and thorough cleaning of items that produce or attract house dust. Unfortunately new dust is constantly being introduced into the air in the home, but to keep it and dust-mites to a minimum, the following suggestions can help.

- Use an ionizer in rooms to decrease air-borne dust.

- Use washable curtains or blinds, and clean them approximately every six weeks.

- Dust with a damp duster to prevent dust from being precipitated into the air.

- Shake your clothes outside, and hang them in a wardrobe, Leaving them on the floor provides an overnight feast for dust-mites.

- If you sleep with a feather duvet or feather pillows, these should be shaken outside every day and left in the sun for no more than 10-15 minutes.

- Once a week, shake cushions and removable components of soft furnishings outside and vacuum* them.

- There are an estimated 2 million dust-mites in the average mattress. To reduce their population, beds should be vacuumed* regularly.

* Most vacuum cleaners stir up dust in the air because particles escape through the bag. See Chapter 11 for information on the Vorwerk vacuum cleaner, which does an exceptionally thorough cleaning job on all surfaces in the home, and filters the air before it is ejected.

RADIATION

Indoor pollution falls into two categories, that which we can see or smell such as smoke or fumes, and pollution which is invisible and produces no odour, such as radiation. The second category can sometimes be the most dangerous because we are unlikely to be aware of its presence. We are surrounded by radiation from natural sources. These include cosmic rays and decay products from certain rocks and soils. Also man-made sources like high-tension power lines, smoke detectors which contain americium 241, X-rays, air travel, luminous clock and watch dials, satellite dishes, television sets and VDUs. We are even exposed to radiation from tobacco smoke, fall-out from nuclear accidents such as Chernobyl, and residual radiation from nuclear weapons testing.

Scientists and doctors are not concerned about an immediate risk to health from radiation, but there is concern about the long-term risk potential, because its effects tend to be cumulative. In the summer when windows are open and there is increased ventilation, any radon seeping into the house from granite will drop considerably. It is usually during the winter months in areas of the country where the bed-rock or the main building material is granite, and the home is well-insulated, that radioactivity can rise to levels which may cause concern. Because radon is invisible and odourless it is impossible to tell whether there is a high level in your home, without special tests. There is no need for concern about the question of radon pollution unless you live in a house constructed from granite, or if you live in some areas of Cornwall, Devon, Derbyshire, or Yorkshire. If you would like more information write, enclosing a stamped addressed envelope to: The Information Officer, National Radiological Protection Board, Chilton, Didcot, Oxon, OX11 0RQ; Telephone: Abingdon (0235) 831600.

In the USA you can obtain a booklet about radiation from: USEPA, Centre for Environmental Protection Information, 26 West St Clair Street, Cincinnati, Ohio 45268.

Protecting Ourselves

Even though we are exposed to many different forms of radiation, it is possible for us to help protect ourselves. Our immune system is our first line of defence and when it is healthy the body can eliminate foreign substances and pathogens. Good nutrition can help the body to protect itself against damage from pollutants, including radiation, and there are specific vitamins and minerals which may play a protective role against the ageing and cancer risks of radiation. Because radiation causes damage by disintegrating molecules and producing free-radicals, we need to supply the body with nutrients that protect cells against free-radical damage, and others which discourage the body from harbouring or taking up dangerous radioactive by-products.

Certain foods and nutrients can have a protective effect against radioactive uptake by the body, and others can bind to radioactive particles and cause their harmless excretion. Nutrients and substances that fall into this category include kelp seaweed, a source of iodine which is taken up by the thyroid gland and prevents it from absorbing radioactive iodine. Sodium alginate from seaweeds, and calcium and magnesium also bind radioactive materials. Foods in the cabbage family, such as Brussels sprouts, red and white cabbage, kale, and mustard greens, can have a protective effect because they contain amino acids which work as antioxidants and poison neutralizers. These detoxifiers bind with radioactive substances, toxins, and heavy metals and excrete them via the urine. The fibre in whole grains and beans can bind with radioactive elements and carry them out of the body through the intestines.

Other nutrients can reduce the cell-damaging oxidant effects of radiation; these are the amino acids glutathione, cystine, and methionine, and vitamins A, C, E, B5, and the mineral selenium. Vitamin A, especially in the form of carotene, can play a double role in protecting the body. Researchers have found that vitamin A can protect the lungs from damage and cancer associated with smoking. As vitamin A is protective to cells in the respiratory system, it may help to guard the lung cells against some of the changes associated with radiation damage. This is an area which requires more study, but it certainly will not hurt to increase your consumption of orange, dark green, and yellow fruit and vegetables.

DIETARY DEFENCE

Vitamins and minerals can be the key to helping the body survive pollution. A good diet protects against chemicals, heavy metal poisoning, and other forms of pollution that we have to live with. It is always best to choose organically grown foods if possible, but if it is difficult, it is still important to include plenty of whole grains and fresh fruit in the diet. Foods also contain other substances that can help the body to detoxify pollutants.

DAILY PROTECTION

✔ Eat plenty of apples, plums, damsons, bananas, and other high pectin foods.

✔ Include seaweeds such as nori, or kelp tablets*. Kelp contains sodium alginate which can help to protect the body against radiation. Sodium alginate combines with strontium 90, a breakdown product of radiation, by acting as a binding agent in the intestine, and causing its excretion from the body.

✔ Eat foods from the cabbage family, garlic, onions, and other sulphur-rich foods such as eggs, and soy lecithin. Garlic contains germanium, and can help the body discharge heavy metal poisoning.

✔ Increase your consumption of fresh orange, dark green and yellow fruit and vegetables. Also include celery, cucumbers, dandelion leaves, and beetroot in the diet. They are good sources of organic sodium which is important for the elimination of poisonous substances from the body. Eat whole grains, sea vegetables, and traditional soy products such as miso, tofu, and tempeh.

✔ Add a little virgin olive oil to your daily salad to increase your intake of essential fatty acids (EFAs).

✔ Herbs such as fennel, sarsaparilla, red clover, slippery elm, horehound, and borage are helpful for eliminating poisons from the body. For more advice contact a herbalist. If you intend to use herbs and are taking any prescription drugs, see *The Medicine Chest* (Thorsons, 1988) to check whether they interact with your medicine. If you are taking a contraceptive pill avoid sarsaparilla.

* Avoid kelp tablets if you are taking thyroid medication, or have any thyroid disorders, unless directed otherwise by your doctor.

☑ Avoid smoking and smoky atmospheres, petrol vapours, eating rancid fats, excessive consumption of sugar, coffee, tea, saturated fats, hydrogenated oils, and refined and processed foods.

☑ A protective daily supplement regime could include 5,000iu of vitamin A from carotene or fish oil, 25-50mg of vitamin B complex, 500mg* of vitamin C and bioflavonoids, 200iu** of vitamin E as natural d-alpha tocopherol, Royal Jelly, 50-100mcg of selenium, and up to 30mg of zinc.

VITAMIN C PROTECTS AGAINST TOBACCO SMOKE AND CHEMICAL FUMES

Vitamin C helps to detoxify pollutants in the body. It is an antioxidant nutrient, which means that it can protect the cells from damage caused by pollution. Vitamin C helps the kidneys and bowels to excrete toxins; it can detoxify carbon monoxide, sulphur dioxide, and cancer-causing substances, and neutralize toxins such as cadmium in tobacco and wood smoke. Vitamin C is particularly important for smokers and those who have to breathe second-hand smoke, because each cigarette smoked, or passively smoked, depletes about 25mg of this nutrient. See Chapter 3 for food sources of vitamin C.

SELENIUM AND VITAMIN E HELP TO PROTECT CELLS AGAINST POLLUTION

Selenium and vitamin E work together as a team. They are known as antioxidants because they can protect the body from oxidation damage to the cells caused by pollutants. Selenium can protect the body against radiation damage, and it has a role in establishing a tolerance to pollutants

* See Checklist 3 in Chapter 7 for important information about vitamin C's interaction with certain medicines.
** Consult your GP before taking vitamin E if you have very high blood pressure, mitral valve stenosis, breast cancer, or are taking heart medication, insulin or medicine for diabetes.

in the environment. The need for both selenium and vitamin E increases when tobacco in all forms is smoked, or during exposure to smoky atmospheres. Chemical sensitivity may be reduced by including plenty of vitamin E and selenium in the diet. For food sources of these nutrients see Chapter 4, Winter Food Power.

VITAMIN A PROTECTS THE LUNGS AND THE CELLS FROM POLLUTANTS

Vitamin A, especially in the form of beta carotene found in orange, yellow and green vegetables and fruit, protects the body from carcinogens, cancer causing substances. It is particularly helpful for protecting the lungs against inhaled pollutants, especially cigarette smoke. It is also an antioxidant and can help to protect the cells against oxidation damage caused by pollutants.

B-COMPLEX VITAMINS HELP THE BODY TO NEUTRALIZE CHEMICALS

Exposure to sulphur dioxide increases the need for B-complex vitamins. B-complex vitamins help to neutralize chemical poisons in the body.

ZINC, CALCIUM AND MAGNESIUM HELP THE BODY TO EXCRETE TOXINS

All the minerals are important for helping the body deal with pollutants, but three of the most important are zinc, calcium and magnesium. Zinc helps to carry heavy metals through the body so that they are harmlessly excreted. It is important for people who are exposed to a high level of lead, such as that from vehicle exhaust, and for smokers. Calcium is important for influencing immunity to cancer, and it can protect the body against radiation. Magnesium is essential for helping the body to dispose of ammonia, a chemical found in cigarette smoke, and it can also help in the elimination of lead from the body. For food sources of these minerals see Chapter 3.

25-POINT PLAN FOR A HEALTHIER HOME ENVIRONMENT

✔ Avoid burning colour newspapers or magazines in the fireplace. It can liberate lead from the inks into the air and this is especially dangerous for children, and anyone confined to the room, especially when there is inadequate ventilation.

✔ Never burn plastics; the fumes liberated by burning are particularly toxic.

✔ If you are allergic to moulds, place a layer of crushed stones on top of the soil in houseplant pots; it will inhibit the growth of mould. Avoid wicker baskets as plant holders, as they can harbour mould.

✔ If you have children or pets, avoid keeping poisonous houseplants such as philodendrons or dieffenbachias. When decorating for Christmas, place holly and mistletoe up high enough to prevent children from reaching them.

✔ Choose wallpaper paste without chemical mould-inhibitors. Mix borax with the paste to inhibit mould without filling the room with chemicals.

✔ Use photoelectric smoke detectors rather than those which contain the radioactive material americium 241.

✔ Don't become an amateur chemist by mixing bleach with either ammonia or toilet cleaners. The result will be a very dangerous gas.

✔ Winter is not the time to give your house a face-lift. Save major indoor painting jobs, and other projects which require adhesives or chemicals, for the spring or summer when windows can be left open for extended periods.

✔ If you cook with a gas oven, ventilate the room well, and if possible, use an extractor fan to remove nitrogen dioxide from the air.

✔ The kitchen and the bathroom both require the highest level of ventilation in the house because of pollution from heating appliances, condensation, stored household cleaners and chemicals.

✔ Have gas appliances fitted by an installer registered with the Confederation for the Registration of Gas Installers (CORGI). All gas appliances should be checked and serviced regularly. Carry out a regular inspection of appliance flues and chimneys, watch for cracks and leaks.

✔ Check chimneys regularly and remove any obstructions such as nests, rubble and other debris. Have chimneys swept regularly and burn 'smokeless' fuel.

✔ Never close wall or ceiling ventilators in kitchens or bathrooms. These are designed to vent gases from boilers, water heaters and other appliances.

✔ Ensure adequate ventilation where gas and paraffin heaters are used.

✔ In confined, poorly ventilated areas, try to avoid smoking and smokers, or use an ionizer to clean the air.

✔ When using paints, solvents, and other chemicals, ventilate the area well and try to avoid sleeping in a newly painted bedroom for up to a week. Most paints can take weeks to dry completely and stop exuding toxic fumes.

✔ Store aerosols and non-biodegradable cleaning products in a garden shed, or a very well ventilated area. Do not expose aerosols to heat such as sunlight, and avoid storing them under a sink where hot or boiling water runs. Better still, avoid using aerosols, and change to natural cleansing products, washing powders etc.

✔ To clean indoor air, use a new-style ionizer that conforms to wiring safety standards — in Britain BS 3456.

✔ Avoid breathing the air around hot showers, baths, washing machines and dryers. These areas should be very well ventilated.

☑ Use a humidifier when the heat is on, but clean it every week because mould can grow in it. and may lead to allergies in sensitive individuals. Scrub the water chamber well with hot water and borax.

☑ Sunshine is naturally antibacterial. Rugs, mattresses and bedding can be placed in the sun for 30 minutes every day to prevent the growth of bacteria and moulds. Place them 'bottom up' so that the colours do not fade.

☑ Dust with a water-dampened cloth to avoid precipitating settled dust back into the air.

☑ If your garage is under the house, avoid putting your car away until the engine has cooled down. Exhaust and gases from the hot engine can seep into your home and could be detrimental to health.

☑ Keep ordinary bottles of perfume, and soft plastic items, out of your bedroom.

☑ Open windows and ventilate all rooms for at least half an hour every day.

BIBLIOGRAPHY

Walter T. Hughes MD, Thomas Kalmer MD, 'Talcum Powder and Children', *American Journal of Diseases of Children* 111, pp.653-4, 1966.

Key Nam MD, Douglas R. Gracey MD, 'Pulmonary Talcosis From Cosmetic Talcum Powder', *Journal of The American Medical Association* 5, Vol.221, 31 July 1972.

'Office Sickness', *Economist* 298, p.77, 8 February 1986.

'Sick Building Syndrome', *Sunday Times*, 26 June 1988.

'Exposure to Chemicals', *Journal of The American Medical Association*, 18 December 1981.

'Deadly Gas', *New Scientist*, 5 Feb. 1987, p.33.

'A Citizen's Guide to Radon', United States Environmental Protection Agency, August 1986.

'Living with Radiation', National Radiological Protection Board, 1988.

'Pollution in the Car', *New Scientist* 1525, p.17. 11 Sept. 1986.

'Radon Risks Spread', *New Scientist* 1617, p.31, 16 June 1988.

B.T. Jones and R.H. Loiselle, 'Reversibility of Serotonin Irritation Syndrome with Atmospheric Anions', *Journal of Clinical Psychiatry* 47, pp.141-143, 1986.

A.P. Kreuger, R.J. Reed, 'Biological Impact of Small Air Ions', *Science* 93, pp.1209-11, 1976.

R. Pratt, R.W. Barnard, 'Some Effects of Ionized Air on Penicillium Notatum', *American Pharmacological Association*, Scientific Edition 49, pp.643-6, 1960.

A.P. Kreuger, R.F. Smith, 'The Biological Mechanism of Air-Ion Action', *Journal of General Physiology* 44, pp.269-76, 1960.

Chapter 5

LET'S GET PHYSICAL

Winter weather is a very good excuse for not exercising; there are so many legitimate reasons for avoiding it. Exercising can be unpleasant, or even dangerous, on very cold, wet, and windy days, especially when there is ice on the pavements. Breathing quantities of cold air can make your throat hurt, and the lungs seize, and jogging in a traffic-filled town or city is more detrimental than beneficial to your health because exercise increases respiration and, therefore raises the intake of hazardous pollutants like carbon monoxide and lead.

Henry Ford thought that exercise was 'bunk'. He claimed that if you were healthy, you did not need it, and if you were sick, you should avoid it, and to back up his point, he produced cars. Most people who dislike exercise will whole-heartedly agree with Mr Ford; however, the following medically and scientifically proven points are food for thought.

- Inactivity increases blood pressure, heart-rate, and susceptibility to depression.

- Inactivity decreases muscle strength, the lungs' ability to absorb oxygen, and the immune system's ability to fight infections.

- Inactivity can make your joints stiff, and the bones may begin to degenerate.

The trouble is, our bodies are intended for movement and activity, and when our lifestyle becomes sedentary we usually pay for it with a decline in physical and emotional health. The answer, then, is to find the right personal exercises that are pleasant and convenient, can be performed in spare moments, and do not reduce you to a state of apathetic boredom after two weeks. This chapter can help you to decide which type(s) of exercise suit you and your lifestyle the best. The suggestions in this chapter are not intended to turn you into a muscular athlete; the aim is purely to find pleasant, enjoyable and realistic ways of increasing your activity and, consequently, your health, during the winter.

THE BENEFITS OF EXERCISE

Even moderate exercise boosts circulation to all parts of the body, including arms, hands, legs and feet. This is a great help to people who feel the cold in the winter.

Most researchers agree that regular 15–20 minute sessions of exercise, that increase pulse and breathing rates to just under double those of resting, contribute immediate and long-term health benefits.

- Activity increases blood flow, which in turn increases body temperature.

- The number of infection-fighting white blood cells in the bloodstream is raised as a result of exercise. White blood cells produce an agent called endogenous pyrogen, which acts on the temperature-regulating centre in the brain and stimulates a rise in body temperature. A slightly raised temperature is hostile to micro-organisms.

- Exercise increases circulation and respiration, encourages the removal of wastes and toxins via the lungs, kidneys and lymph, and increases the efficiency and capacity of the heart and lungs.

- Normal pulse rate and blood pressure are lowered.

- Bones become stronger and denser because minerals are utilized more efficiently and mineralization is encouraged. Muscle tone is also improved, and tendons, ligaments and joints become stronger and more flexible.

- The brain and central nervous system benefit from the extra intake of oxygen and enhanced circulation caused by exercise. This can improve concentration, short-term memory, and decrease depression.

- Exercise moderates fat and cellulite.
- Energy levels improve and become more stable.

INACTIVITY

The visible signs of an inactive lifestyle are the development of flabby areas of the body caused by unused muscles losing their tone. This is often evident in people who sit at a desk all day, and it usually appears around the buttocks and thighs, a problem known by American women as 'the saddle-bag syndrome'. Another complication caused by prolonged sitting is the possibility of developing varicose veins. Muscle action pumps blood through the veins, but during inactivity the heart has to do all the work. Sitting for hours every day interferes with the proper flow of blood because the edges of chairs restrict the vessels and this can eventually lead to varicosities. The invisible effects of prolonged lack of exercise tend to be more subtle and usually do not occur as noticeable problems until they require medical attention. These can include high blood pressure, decreased lung and heart capacity, increased blood fat levels, and even unwarranted depression.

Many of us spend such a large percentage of winter days indoors that our need for exercise is often not met. Housework can be tiring, but being busy does not necessarily provide the kind of exercise which promotes energy and stamina.

A fast-paced work schedule is more likely to create stress, fatigue, and irritability, rather than cause healthy stimulation of the cardiovascular system, relieving tension, and promoting fitness.

Our bodies function best when circulation is stimulated by the type of movement which causes a healthy stress on the heart, increases breathing and oxygen intake, and tones all our organs and muscles; regular aerobic type exercises will achieve this.

FITNESS

The advantages of 'being fit' are numerous and affect many areas of your life. Fitness can be measured by how well you sleep and how refreshed you feel in the morning, whether or not you ache or feel stiff after exercise, how good your usual energy level is, how cheerful you generally feel, how you handle everyday stress, and how out of breath you are after running for a bus or walking up stairs. The better your answers to these points, the fitter you are likely to be.

YOUR FINGER ON THE PULSE

Exercise is most beneficial when the heart and pulse rate is raised to a little under double that of resting. To find out what your normal resting pulse is, sit and relax for about five minutes, then take either your right or left hand and place your thumb on your chin so that your hand is resting on your neck. With your fingers together, move your hand until you can feel your pulse. Time yourself for 30 seconds while you count the pulse beats. Multiply the number you arrive at by two and this will give you your pulse/heart-rate for one minute.

The average resting pulse/heart-rate for men is 72 beats a minute, and for women, 80 beats a minute.

If you are over 40 and have not exercised for a while, have recently been ill, or have any heart disorders, rheumatic fever, high blood pressure, chest pains, or severe diabetes, you should contact your doctor before increasing your normal activity. It is always far safer and more productive to exercise regularly, and gradually increase the duration of the activity rather than the intensity.

To find your optimum exercise heart-rate, subtract your age from 195. The resulting figure is your most beneficial exercise heart-rate per minute.

In order to check your exercise heart and pulse rate, take your pulse for ten seconds immediately after exercising, and multiply the number obtained by six. It is important not to count beyond ten seconds as the heart-rate will be slowing down and the reading will be inaccurate.

Correct breathing is important, but during some types of exercise your natural instinct may be to hold your breath. Because all the cells and tissues in the body benefit from the increased intake of oxygen which exercise stimulates, incorrect breathing while exercising can defeat its purpose. Always check that you are breathing properly whenever you do any exercises.

EXERCISE FOR THE WHOLE FAMILY

Successful exercising, like proper nutrition, involves variety, and the different types of exercise in this chapter are included so that the right ones can be chosen by every member of the family, no matter how young, old or busy. Different activities suit different people best, so consult the table on page 104 to see which forms of exercise may be the most enjoyable and easy for you.

> An elderly person will feel more of the fatigue caused by effort 24–48 hours later, and consequently it is easy to go beyond capabilities before being aware of having done so.

If you are elderly, always stop exercising well before you feel that you have done enough. This can help to prevent the danger of exhaustion and stiffness developing one or two days after any unaccustomed activity or physical exercise. Avoid stressing one particular joint, and if any area feels stiff, make the movements very slow and gentle. Never exercise to the point of pain.

Deciding when to exercise is mainly a matter of personal choice, but it is important to find the right kind of exercise to fit in with any spare time. Always avoid exercising immediately before or after eating — it is best to take any strenuous activity at least 15 minutes before, or two hours after a meal. Try to aim for at least three or four exercise sessions a week, each one lasting for about 15–20 minutes.

WINTER EXERCISES — THE RIGHT CHOICES

Category	Some choices
Muscular body, heavy bone structure	Court sports, judo, wrestling, boxing, cycling, swimming, walking, weight training , rebounding, slant-board exercises.
Lean body, light bone structure	Walking, swimming, running, court sports, fencing, skating, gymnastics, rebounding.
Rounder body, more fat than muscle	Walking, swimming, cycling, golf, archery, slant-board exercises, rebounding.

As a general rule, if you are over 40, have recently been ill, rarely exercise, have diabetes, or any kind of heart condition or very high blood pressure, contact your doctor for advice before attempting anything more strenuous than a gentle walk.

There should always be a warm-up period and a cooling-down period whenever you exercise. Sudden and strenuous activity can damage muscles, so a warm-up routine will ensure they are relaxed. Warm muscles move more easily, without the risk of sprain or strain. Also, warming up allows the body temperature to rise gently, and as muscles warm up they demand more oxygen which naturally stimulates heart-rate to increase and pump more oxygen-rich blood to the muscles.

After moderate to strenuous exercise it is important to cool down because this gradually takes the strain off the heart, and also helps to avoid post-exercise stiffness by ensuring that waste acids are pumped away from the extremities.

Only exercise until pleasantly tired. You should be breathless rather than speechless.

If you are fighting an infection and your usual exercise routine becomes difficult, relax, don't do it! Stress decreases immune response. Exercise requires strong lung function, and if the respiratory tract is constricted, or filled with mucus, then the heart and lungs will become quickly fatigued, because they will be working harder to circulate oxygen throughout the body. Never exercise if you have a fever. Your body needs to conserve energy, and the increased temperature generated by exercise could be cumulative, resulting in heat exhaustion.

INCREASING INDOOR EXERCISE

Staying indoors during the winter decreases the amount of day-to-day exercise that we are normally exposed to, so in addition to the exercises outlined in this chapter there are some very simple, low-effort steps which can be taken to boost indoor activity. Even a little extra exercise is good for your health.

- Put the remote-control for the television out of reach. Walk over and change the channel.

- Place the telephone on the opposite side of the room from your chair. Put a slant-board by the telephone and take advantage of some refreshing but restful exercise while you carry on your conversation. For more information see A New Slant on Health in this chapter.

- If you are in good health, jog up the stairs instead of walking.

- At work, or if you live in flats, avoid the lift and use the stairs if you are not carrying anything too heavy.

- Try using natural beeswax polish on your furniture. It takes more effort to bring out the shine and the benefits include extra upper body exercises (change hands as you work to exercise both sides of your body), and the avoidance of aerosol chemicals in the air. For more information about indoor pollution see Chapter 4.

- Pursuing an enjoyable hobby can add exercise benefits — even knitting uses more energy than just slumping in front of the television.

WINTER AT WORK — BEATING THE EXERCISE PROBLEM

Headaches, neckaches, joint soreness, stiffness, back pains, muscle aches, numb thighs and feet, varicose veins, fatigue, weight gain, constipation, stress, and fatigue — these are all common complaints suffered by thousands of people with jobs that require long periods of sitting. They are frequently a direct result of inactivity, lack of fresh air, and remaining seated for hours at a time. Aches and pains are often worse in the winter because it is harder to exercise outside; lunch-breaks are frequently spent in the canteen, sitting in the staff room, or remaining at the desk.

REDUCING TENSION AND LOOSENING STIFF JOINTS

The following exercises can be performed while sitting. Begin very slowly and gently, and only do the repeats when you have become used to the stretches. It is important never to overdo new exercises because it is easy to pull muscles. Avoid exercising soon after eating and always allow at least two hours to elapse after a meal.

1 This stretch can be carried out while sitting or standing. Link your fingers together and raise your arms above your head with your palms towards the ceiling. Reach as high as you can and hold the stretch for a count of ten. Repeat, but this time tilt your arms slightly to the left, hold for a count of ten, then repeat the stretch with your arms tilted to the right.

2 Lower your chin onto your chest. Clasp your hands together and rest them on the back of your head. Stretch gently and hold for a count of ten. Drop your arms down to your sides then rest your head on your right shoulder, keeping your shoulders straight, stretch so that you can feel a gentle pull on the left side of your neck and hold for a count of ten. Repeat this stretch with your neck resting on your left shoulder. Lastly, leave your arms relaxed by your side, then tip your head backwards and hold the stretch for a count of ten.

3 Sit up straight in your chair, let your arms relax by your sides, and squeeze your shoulder blades back, in towards each other, and up towards your ears. Hold for a count of five and then lower them down as far as

they will go. Repeat up to five times and finish with your shoulders relaxed.

4 Stand or sit in a clear area. Gently swing your right arm in a clockwise direction up to ten times, and then anticlockwise up to ten times. Repeat the exercise with your left arm.

5 Sit up tall in your chair with your arms out straight in front of you, then turning slowly, twist your upper body, waist, and arms to the right and then to the left.

6 Place your hands on your thighs and then rotate both shoulders together. Repeat up to ten times forwards and then backwards.

7 Sit on a comfortable chair, hold your legs out in front of you, and circle both feet and ankles to the right and then to the left. Repeat this in each direction about five times.

8 Place your hands on your shoulders and move your elbows up, back, and down, in a circular motion. Repeat up to ten times, and then repeat up to ten times in the opposite direction.

CHAIR AND DESK ISOMETRICS

Isometric exercises involve using groups of muscles in opposition, which increases circulation and strength, and brings about relaxation. Isometrics can be performed in a small or confined space, and to benefit from them it is not necessary to repeat the exercises more than once a day.

Isometrics are simple but powerful exercises that can be done by almost everyone; however, they should be avoided if you have heart disorders or high blood pressure. Before attempting any of the exercises, consult your doctor, osteopath, or chiropractor if you are receiving treatment for any back or spinal disorders.

Upper Body

Inhale slowly and deeply while raising both arms above your head with your hands positioned so that the 'heels' of your hands are touching. Breathe out slowly and push against your left hand with your right, while resisting the pressure with your left arm. Hold for a count of five. Bring your arms down to your sides, then repeat the exercise reversing the push and resistance to the opposite arms.

Abdominal Muscles, Arms and Shoulders

This isometric exercise can be performed at a desk or table which is approximately 5 feet (150 cm) wide. Place your chair in a central position, then sit with your back straight and hold on to both sides of the desk or table. Pull inwards strongly, as if you were trying to fold the table top up, and at the same time inhale slowly and deeply. Hold for a count of five seconds, then exhale as you slowly release your pull. Repeat the exercise twice, maintaining a good posture.

Chest and Thighs

Sit on the edge of your chair with your feet flat on the floor. Lean over and place both hands on the inside of your knees. Inhale slowly and deeply, and as you exhale try to bring your knees together as you resist with your hands. Hold for a count of ten.

RELAXING AND REVIVING EXERCISES

1 Stand up tall with your arms stretched above your head. Breathe in slowly and deeply, hold the breath for a count of five, and then, as you slowly breathe out, bend forwards at the waist and allow your body and arms to relax; hold for a count of five. Repeat up to five times. This exercise is relaxing and increases the circulation of blood to the head and brain.

2 Sit comfortably, then close off your right nostril with your thumb or index finger while you take a deep, slow breath in through your left nostril. Hold your breath for a count of five then block your left nostril and breathe out through your right. Repeat five times, then reverse the technique by breathing in through your left nostril and out through your right. This is a good energizer, but it should be avoided if you work in a very smoky, dusty, chemical-laden, or dirty area.

TIPS FOR A HAPPIER, HEALTHIER WINTER AT WORK

- Fresh air is important throughout the day, and remember to open a window while you carry out any indoor exercises. If this is not possible, it would help to install an ionizer in your work area to clear smoke and dust from the air. For more details about ionizers see Chapter 4.

- If the heating in your work area dries the air, consider using a humidifier. If this is not possible, a cup of steaming water on the desk, or a surface close to you, will help to humidify the air a little.

- Your chair should be adjustable so that you are at the right height and position for your work. This can help to reduce neck- and backaches.

- A wedge cushion placed on your chair seat, thick end to the back and thin end to the front, will tilt you slightly forwards and relieve some of the pressure on your spine.

- Restrictive clothing, or waistbands which feel tight around your middle, cut off circulation, restrict digestion, hinder breathing, and can make you feel uncomfortable all day.

- Getting up and moving approximately every half hour helps to get the circulation going, and prevents stiff and aching joints.

- During breaks, a rebounder can be used to increase circulation and respiration. For more information see Bouncing with Health in this chapter. Try to go out for a walk at lunchtime, if the weather permits.

- An osteopath or chiropractor can relieve work-induced neck- and backaches and will help you to find out why you are suffering from them, and what you can do to prevent them. Sometimes your employer will pay for the treatment — it is worth enquiring. To find a practitioner in your area see Chapter 11.

A DIFFERENT SLANT ON HEALTH

We are all under the influence of gravity, which exerts a downward pull on our entire body including the heart, blood flow, and organs. After a hard day at work, especially during the winter when we tend to get less exercise, our ability to resist the pull of gravity decreases, and the result may be fatigue, lack of mental clarity, and bad circulation.

> By changing the position of your body so that the pull of gravity is reversed, you feel fresher, more energetic, and relaxed.

Lying on a slant-board reverses the gravitational pull on the organs and encourages them to return to their natural positions. Nerve and blood flow is also naturally improved. The flow of oxygen and nutrient-rich blood is increased to the head and brain, which enhances mental clarity.

Ten minutes relaxing with your feet raised higher than your head can be equivalent to resting for half an hour when lying flat.

HOW TO MAKE A SLANT-BOARD

To make a slant-board you will need a wooden board about ¾-inch (2cm) thick, 6 feet (180cm) long, and 18 inches (45cm) wide. Cover the board with dense padding, and lay cotton towelling over it as an outer cover. To secure the padding and cover, pull the fabric taut and attach it to the sides or bottom of the board with short, flat-headed nails which will not penetrate through to the surface where you will be lying. Fix one end, very securely, about 18 inches (45cm) above the floor. Make a foot strap, about 6 inches (15cm) down from the top of the raised end, by attaching a 2 inch (5cm) wide piece of fabric or an old belt. Secure the ends to the sides, or underneath the board, with short, flat-headed nails.

If you are unable to make a slant-board, an old bed headboard which is three quarters of an inch thick or an ironing board will probably work, but beware of any exposed nails, and if your ironing board has an asbestos mat, or is not very sturdy, do not use it. Fold the ironing board up so that it is flat. Raise one end up, approximately eighteen inches, and secure it so that it will not tip or fall; the other end should rest on the floor. If you are using a headboard make sure that the raised end is well secured to prevent it from falling.

When you are absolutely certain that the board is secure, you can lie on it so that your head is at the lower end and your feet are raised. You will benefit from this whether you carry out exercises or just relax for a few minutes.

SLANT-BOARD RELAXATION

Use the slant-board up to three times a day and choose moments when you can relax peacefully. The best times to use a slant-board are before lunch, around three in the afternoon, and in the evening before going to bed, but always wait at least two hours after a meal.

To help clear your mind while you relax try listening to some soft music, or a radio broadcast. Allow yourself ten minutes for each session. If you telephone friends in the afternoon or the evening, try placing the slant-board by the telephone, and relax, or exercise on it while you are talking. It is surprising how clear your thinking becomes.

SLANT-BOARD EXERCISES

Exercises done on a slant-board are particularly beneficial because the pull of gravity is reversed, and circulation is improved. They will help to tone and strengthen areas of your body which may be difficult to exercise, especially the underarms, inner thighs and other regions which tend to get a little flabby as we get older.

Warning

None of the exercises should be performed vigorously. Do them slowly and gently, and gradually build up to the repetitions suggested.

Only use a slant-board with your doctor's consent if you have any heart disease, uterine haemorrhage, high blood pressure, back or spinal disorders, cancer, are pregnant, have recently had surgery, or are suffering from any serious illness.

1 Lie on the board with your toes tucked under the foot strap. Raise your arms above your head and stretch your whole body, holding for a count of five. Relax and repeat the stretch.

2 Raise your arms above your head, hold for a count of two and then

bring them down to your sides. Repeat the exercise up to ten times. To increase the value of this exercise it can be done using light hand weights of approximately 2-5 lb (1-2kg).

3 With your left arm down by your side, raise your right arm above your head. Hold for a count of two, and then bring your right arm to your side and raise your left arm above your head. Repeat with both arms up to ten times. This exercise may also be carried out using 2-5 lb (1–2kg) hand weights.

4 Lie flat on the board with your arms by your sides. Relax, then lift your back and buttocks off the board so that your weight rests on your shoulders. Hold for a count of five then relax. Repeat the exercise as many times as is comfortable — up to five.

5 Lie flat on the board with your arms by your sides and hands gripping the edges. Slip your feet out of the toe strap and raise both legs straight into the air. Gently pull your legs apart so that they form a 'V'. Only extend them until you begin to feel a slight pull in your inner thighs. Avoid 'bouncing' your legs apart. Hold for a count of five and bring them back together. Repeat up to five times.

6 Raise your legs into the air and move them in a slow, gentle bicycling motion, counting one, and two, and three etc., up to ten.

7 This last exercise should not be attempted if you have any spinal disorders, and is only to be attempted if you are relatively fit. Lie flat on the board with your arms by your sides. Tuck your feet under the toe strap and gently raise your upper body to a sitting position, without the aid of your hands. Hold for a count of two, and then very slowly bring your body back onto the board. If you can only raise your body a little way this is perfectly all right. It will still help to strengthen your abdominal muscles, and with time you will find that the exercise becomes much easier.

8 Slip your feet out of the two straps and relax for one or two minutes. To prevent dizziness when rising, place both feet on the floor at the sides of the board, and then gradually raise your body to a sitting position. Stand up slowly.

BOUNCING WITH HEALTH

If you are a firm believer that exercise is boring, then rebounding may be the one form of exercise which can convince you otherwise. The following questions and answers will help you to decide whether rebounding is for you.

What on earth is rebounding?

Rebounding is classed as an aerobic exercise, along with running, fast walking, swimming, skipping, cycling etc. It is a rhythmical activity which increases respiration, heart-rate and muscle metabolism. It is performed on a mini-relation of the trampoline, known as a rebounder, which is an eight-footed circular frame with a bouncy mat, suspended about eight inches from the ground by strong springs. These are covered with a plastic trim to protect your toes. The sturdy legs all have non-slip rubber caps to prevent both you and the rebounder from migrating to the other side of the room during a particularly energetic bouncing session.

Are there any situations when it would be unhealthy to rebound?

Almost everyone in good health, from the young to the elderly, should be able to enjoy rebounding because it can be performed at a level which suits the individual. Very gentle exercise is almost always beneficial, but check with your doctor if you are concerned that you should not increase your activity, or if you suffer from any type of heart disease, or diabetes which is complicated with severe metabolic problems; if you have been very ill within the last few months, have had an operation or medical procedure recently; or if you have a prolapsed uterus.

If you have high blood pressure, consult your doctor about which types of exercise and how much you can attempt. The right exercise is very beneficial because it can help to lower blood pressure and, in fact, it may be lowered for several hours after aerobic type exercises such as walking or rebounding. The benefit is due to exercise increasing the diameter of the blood vessels, which allows blood to flow under less pressure.

One of the advantages of using a rebounder is that you do not have to exercise strenuously to derive benefit, and this means that you may be able to use a rebounder very gently during the early stages of pregnancy, but only if your doctor agrees.

As a general rule, before attempting any form of exercise, especially if you do not exercise regularly, begin very slowly, and gradually build up your effort over a number of weeks.

Avoid rebounding immediately before you eat or for two hours after a meal, especially if you exercise quite energetically. Rebounding close to eating could upset your digestion and make you feel sick or give you stomach cramps.

How do you rebound?

Place the rebounder either indoors or outside. Choose some music which makes you feel like dancing because this can help you to keep a steady rhythm. Music with a medium tempo is often best, especially while you are getting used to rebounding. If it is too fast it could be difficult to stay with the rhythm and you may lose your balance. In order to stay on the mat, especially if you are new to rebounding, fix your eyes on an object, or a mark on the wall, and this will help to keep you steady.

Like all forms of exercise, a gentle warm-up period is always necessary. Warm muscles respond most efficiently; when muscles are taut or cold there is more chance of injury or strain. Warm up on a rebounder by walking on the spot, then gradually begin a bouncing jog with the feet barely leaving the mat. Swing your arms gently while doing these warm-ups, and consciously begin to let your body relax. Avoid holding your breath and become aware of breathing properly. Do this for up to a minute, relax and then try it for another minute. At the end of each exercise session cool down by gently bouncing for a minute or two in order to bring the heart-rate back to normal.

As you become used to rebounding there are many exercises that can be performed and new ideas can be included as you progress. A chart of exercises is provided with the PT Bouncer (see Chapter 11).

If you rebound in an upstairs room make sure that the floorboards are strong enough to take the stress, and avoid placing the rebounder right in the middle of the room, especially if you are quite heavy. If you have very low ceilings and you are tall, or incorporate high-jumps into your routine, be careful not to hit your head on the ceiling or dislodge the light fixtures!

There are no special clothes required for rebounding, although it is always important to avoid any clothing which restricts your movements. Wearing a bra is important to prevent breast tissue damage, especially if your rebound programme is quite vigorous.

Will rebounding help my general health?

Rebounding has the potential to exercise the whole body, but it goes a step further because bouncing on a rebounder changes the gravitational pull on the body. At the top point of each bounce you become free of gravity for a split second, just like the weightlessness encountered by astronauts.

The gravity-free period, and the increased pull of gravity experienced when you land back on the mat, along with the acceleration and deceleration of bouncing up and down, bring about rhythmical changes in your body's exposure to the force of gravity. This may not sound very exciting, but within your body these changes exert a healthy stress on the cells, strengthening them, and increasing their capacity to carry out all their vital functions, including the excretion of wastes. The cells also benefit from the increased intake of oxygen brought about by enhanced respiration.

Winter weather can leave you feeling fatigued and tired, but this may be overcome with regular rebounding. Exercise, including rebounding, stimulates your metabolism and glands and increases the intake of revitalizing oxygen. General circulation is improved by exercise, and gentle rebounding has special advantages for the elderly, especially when circulation is bad and the cold is felt easily.

Regular rebounding improves the capacity and efficiency of the heart, blood vessels and lungs, helps to build endurance, strengthens muscles and cells, and aids the body in the elimination of wastes, some of which may have been stored as cellulite.

Exercise decreases blood levels of cholesterol and triglycerides because the levels of low-density lipoprotein (LDL) are lowered, and high-density lipoprotein (HDL) are raised. High-density lipoprotein is a useful blood fat which helps the body to eliminate harmful fats. However, to have a positive effect on blood fats, researchers believe that you need about 20–60 minutes of exercise three times a week, of the kind which raises the heart/pulse-rate. Regular rebound sessions every day should also have a positive effect on blood fats.

Exercise has a positive effect on the digestive system. It stimulates the production of gastric juices so foods are better digested and absorbed, and it also helps the body to eliminate wastes.

Rebounding can have great psychological advantages for people who usually find it difficult to exercise. Hospitals and physiotherapists are using rebounders to help patients recover from certain operations, or to help conditions such as arthritis. For people who have a severe handicap which prevents them from moving their legs, a physiotherapist can provide the 'bounce' while the legs are resting on the rebounder, this produces movement which helps circulation. If you wish to try this form of exercise/physiotherapy, it is important to discuss it with your doctor and physiotherapist.

The central nervous system is positively affected by regular exercise, and mental performance and alertness are raised because of increased circulation and oxygen to all parts of the body including the brain.

Rebound exercise wakes up the lymph system and increases its flow. One of the functions of the lymph is to transport cellular wastes out of the body, and because it needs muscle movement to make it pump, the bouncing exercise and the anti-gravity factor, plus acceleration and deceleration are extremely beneficial in helping the lymph to drain.

Does rebounding help you to lose weight?

Exercise on a rebounder can help weight loss, in conjunction with a good diet, because it helps to increase the metabolism and burns calories. Even after rebounding, the metabolism continues to run at an increased rate for a while, so the energy-burning benefits continue. Muscles use fat as fuel during aerobic exercise, and rebounding also raises the pulse rate which enhances the amount of oxygen supplied to the cells via the lungs.

More oxygen means that the body is able to burn more calories. It is believed that fat loss can continue for more than a year after exercise is increased.

Dieting without exercise is rarely the answer to weight loss because the body does its best to hold on to any fat reserves it has built up — probably even more so in the winter.

If you are seriously overweight please consult your doctor before attempting to rebound. If your doctor consents, then exercise should be started very slowly and gently, and gradually built up over a period of time.

My young children have taken over my rebounder, but should they be rebounding?

Young children love rebounding and it is an excellent and enjoyable way for them to develop coordination and strength. Children should be supervised to prevent the possibility of a fall, although a rebounder is rarely more than 8 inches (20cm) high. If you have two enthusiastic young bouncers they should never rebound together because the heaviest child could bounce the lighter one off the rebounder.

I am over 65 and don't exercise very much; should I try rebounding?

Talk to your doctor before attempting to rebound, especially if you exercise infrequently. Gentle rebounding, with your doctor's consent, can have numerous health benefits, and whether you are 25, or 85, the heart, nervous system, and muscles all respond well to aerobic exercise. Regular rebounding is particularly helpful after retirement because this is often the time when activity decreases, and less exercise can lead to an increased possibility of bone fractures. Exercise improves bone density.

Always remember that the intensity of any exercise you do is not so important as how regularly you do it. As you become used to the exercise, very gradually begin to increase the time you spend exercising, but not the intensity.

The rebounder acts as a shock absorber and prevents the chance of injury or stress to the joints. If you feel that you need some support for better balance, a support-bar can be added to the larger version of the PT Bouncer. For more details of the PT Bouncer see Chapter 11.

BIBLIOGRAPHY

A.D. Simons, C.R. McGownan, L.H. Epstein, D.J. Kupfer, R.J. Robertson, 'Exercise As a Treatment of Depression: an update', *Psychological Reviews* 5:553–68, 1985.

E.W. Martinsen, A. Medhus, L. Sandvik, 'Effects of Aerobic Exercise on Depression, a Complete Study', *British Medical Journal* 291:109, 1985.

J.A. Muir, M.D. Gray, M.R.C.G.P., M.R.C.P., F.F.C.M., 'Physical Fitness — the Key to Good Health', *Geriatric Medicine* 17, 6, pp. 35–39, June 1987.

Chapter 6

MOOD MEDICINE

THE WINTER OF OUR DISCONTENT

For millions of people, there is something depressing about the shorter days of autumn and winter. A grey mental gloom settles over them with clockwork regularity as soon as the days draw in and the mornings get darker. For a percentage of the population, this acts as an unseen magnet, drawing them to the travel agents to book mood-boosting, sun-drenched holidays. For others it is a sign to go into semi-hibernation because they are unable to function normally.

IN THE DARK

At the beginning of the twentieth century, about three-quarters of the population worked outside in natural daylight. In the 1930s and early 1940s the figures began to fall, and by 1964 only 5 million people worked on the land. Twenty years later this figure had plummeted to 1.8 million out of the UK population of almost 57 million.

> About 97 per cent of the population now work indoors, with a growing reliance on artificial light. Because of the way working hours are set up, there are some people who do not see natural daylight for five days of the week, three months of the year.

Lack of daylight can make people feel mildly depressed and mentally less acute, but it can have a more profound effective on the health and well-being of a small section of the population. The medically recognized seasonal affective disorder, aptly named SAD, is a recurrent depression which occurs in the winter months, and clears in the spring. It seems to affect more women than men, and is characterized by oversleeping, feelings of coldness and lethargy, craving for carbohydrates, overeating, weight gain, loss of interest in work, and a withdrawal from people, social activities, and sex. It may also be accompanied by irritability. Changes in blood sugar levels lead to depression, tiredness and irritability.

SEEING THE LIGHT

Life on earth is governed by the sun, moon, gravity, and the earth's rotation around the sun. Light is a powerful force, and its internal biochemical effects on our psyche, glandular function, growth, and even our ability to fight infection, are linked with the passage of light through the retina. On its journey through the eye, light passes to the optic nerve, and is directed to the brain's vision centre, and also to the mainspring of the body's internal clock which is located in the hypothalamus. The hypothalamus regulates the glands and hormones, body temperature, intake and output of water, sexual and reproductive functions, appetite control, sleeping and wakefulness. Injury to the hypothalamus may result in emotional outbursts, overeating with obesity, decreased sexual activity, and changes in wakefulness — all symptoms of SAD, which may suggest that the hypothalamus uses sunlight as a driving force.

From the hypothalamus, a nerve transmission generated by the light travels down the brain stem and out of a mass of nerve tissue, which transmits it back into the brain to the pineal gland. This gland is pine-cone shaped, and about the size of a pea. It is the main producer of a sleep-inducing, mood-depressing hormone called melatonin. Melatonin secretion follows a circadian rhythm and is normally released at night in the dark, but not during the day, as light suppresses it.

LIGHT UP YOUR LIFE

A brisk walk in the fresh air and sunlight can lift your mood and dissolve a winter depression, or irritability. It can also decrease cravings for sweet foods.

If you spend most of your time indoors, or wear glass-lensed glasses all day, then your exposure to full spectrum light will probably be outweighed by partial spectrum light. This is because light filtered through glass is missing the more beneficial part of the spectrum.

Light is colour vibrations, and daylight is composed of a full range of colours — wavelengths known as the spectrum. Blue-green light cuts melatonin levels, but violet and red light increase it slightly. The light from ordinary electric bulbs is mainly from the red part of the spectrum, and predominantly yellow-green comes from cool-white fluorescent tubes. Neither of these have the even distribution of spectral colours found in daylight, nor are they a marked source of the ultraviolet or infra-red spectrum also found in natural daylight. The limited spectrum of regular artificial light-sources does not provide the benefits of sunlight or full spectrum light, and it is thought to be responsible for a number of negative effects.

Working indoors all day has many health disadvantages, especially during the winter. Apart from getting outside as much as possible, and opening windows whenever the weather permits, full spectrum light exposure can be 'supplemented' by using an artificial light source that mimics daylight's spectrum (see Chapter 11 under Full Spectrum Lighting for more information). Full spectrum tubes can be used in homes and the workplace, and they benefit health because they follow the intensity and natural spectrum of daylight more closely than any other artificial light source.

Full spectrum lighting does not give you a tan, but its ultraviolet spectrum is important for the immune system, and it does encourage vitamin D synthesis in the skin. This is vitally important, especially to the elderly and vegans or some vegetarians during the darker winter months. Vitamin D aids the body's utilization of calcium, which in turn helps to prevent brittle bones or osteoporosis. For people whose diet excludes all animal foods, the main source of vitamin D in the winter is exposure to sunlight, and as vitamin D is involved in the immune system and in calcium absorption, lack of it could increase vulnerability to certain health problems.

Full spectrum fluorescent light tubes may be connected directly to existing fixtures, and although they cost more than ordinary fluorescent tubes, they last much longer. Working and living under these lights can have a positive effect on mood, health, work efficiency, and alertness. They are also used successfully by doctors in their research on SAD.

Bringing full spectrum light indoors may help to end some of the health and emotional problems suffered by so many people during dull, depressing winters in northern latitudes.

COLOUR YOUR MOOD

The colours you dress in, or surround yourself with, can also affect or reflect mood. Bright colours are stimulating and darker colours sedate.

Pink tones are calming and keep you on an even keel.
Yellow is a cheering colour.
Blue creates a calm, cooling, environment.
Red is heating, revitalizing and stimulating.
Green represents harmony and balance.

MOOD AND FOOD

Although sunshine and fresh air are the best nutrients, occasional and transient bouts of depression may be helped by ensuring that your diet contains a good variety of vitamins and minerals including B-complex. See Chapter 3 for the Food and Nutrients Quick Reference Chart. Avoid sweet, starchy foods, coffee and alcohol which all rob your body of the nutrients it needs for the healthy function of the nervous system. Check Chapter 9 to see whether any medicines you are taking could be depleting particular nutrients.

✔ *Bio Strath* is an excellent tonic and natural supplement of B vitamins and herbs which can be used by the whole family.

✔ Try to eat plenty of foods containing the mood-elevating vitamin B3, or take a B-complex supplement with up to 100mg of extra niacin or nicotinic acid. Niacin supplements cause vasodilation — opening up the blood vessels. This results in a flushing, tingling sensation over the body, and a loss of heat from the skin. Because of this reaction it is advisable to avoid doses over 50-100mg in very cold weather.

✔ Royal jelly is a natural food source of vitamins, minerals, and amino acids. It can also help, especially if your energy level is low.

✔ Evening primrose oil is involved with glands and hormones which can affect mood and energy.

✔ Vitamin C and bioflavonoids are important for the adrenal glands.

✔ Vitamins A and D may be supplemented by taking a daily dose of emulsified cod liver oil.

✔ Magnesium is often found to be low in some types of depression. Ensure that your diet contains plenty of sources of this mineral (see the Nutrients Quick Reference Chart in Chapter 3) and, if necessary, take a supplement of calcium and magnesium.

✔ Low blood sugar can cause feelings of depression and may be helped in some cases with the addition of GTF chromium in supplement form. If you eat a large proportion of sugary foods, or crave them, or if you drink alcohol regularly, you may suffer from occasional bouts of hypoglycaemia — low blood sugar. If you suspect that this may be the case, contact a natural practitioner for individual help.

If you are in the dark about where to find help for winter depression or SAD, see Chapter 11.

BIBLIOGRAPHY

The New Geographical Digest George Philip and Son, 1986.

Central Statistics Office, Annual Abstract of Statistics 1988, HMSO.

'Full Spectrum Classroom Light and Sickness in Pupils', Lancet, 21 Nov. 1987, p.1205.

'Ain't no Cure for the Wintertime Blues — Or is There?', New Scientist, 7 Jan. 1988.

Alfred J. Lewy MD, et al., 'Bright Artificial Light Treatment of a Manic-Depressive Patient with a Seasonal Mood Swing', *American Journal of Psychiatry*, Nov. 1982.

Jane E. Brody, 'Surprising Health Impact Discovered for Light', *New York Times*, 13 November 1984.

Jane E. Brody, 'From Fertility to Mood, Sunlight Found to Affect Human Biology', *Science Times*, New York Times.

M. Abas, D. Murphy, 'Seasonal Affective Disorder', *British Medical Journal*, p.1504, 12 December 1987.

C.J. Hellekson et al., 'Phototherapy for Seasonal Affective Disorder in Alaska', *American Journal of Psychiatry* 143, pp.1035-1037, 1986.

G. Isaacs, D.S. Staineer, T.E. Sensky, S. Moor and C. Thompson, 'Phototherapy and its Mechanism of Action in Seasonal Affective Disorder, *Journal of Affective Disorders* 14, pp.13-19, 1988.

S.P. James et al., 'Treatment of Seasonal Affective Disorder With Light in the Evening', *British Journal of Psychiatry* 147, 1985, pp.424-428.

A.J. Lewy, R.L. Sack, L.S. Miller, and T.M. Hoban, 'Antidepressant and Circadian Phase-Shifting Effects of Light, *Science* 235, 1987.

A.J. Lewy et al., 'Treating Phase Typed Chronobiologic Sleep and Mood Disorders Using Appropriately Timed Bright Artificial Light', *Psychopharm. Bulletin* 21, 1980.

A.J. Lewy et al., 'Light Suppresses Melatonin Secretion in Humans', *Science* 210, p.1267, 1980.

N.E. Rosenthal, et al., 'Seasonal Affective Disorder in Children, and Adolescents', *American Journal of Psychiatry* 143, pp.356-358, 1986.

C. Thompson, G. Isaacs, 'Seasonal Affective Disorder — A British Sample', *Journal of Affective Disorders* 14, pp.1-11, 1988.

Charles A. Ozeisler et al., 'Bright Light Re-Sets the Human Circadian Pacemaker Independent of the Timing of the Sleep-Wake Cycle', *Science* 233, Aug. 1986.

J.S. Goodwin, 'Nutritional Status in a Healthy Elderly Population: Vitamin D', *American Journal of Clinical Nutrition* 36, pp.1225-33, 1982.

M.R. Baker et al., 'The Decline in Vitamin D Status with Age', *Age and Ageing* 9, pp.249-52, 1980.

A.M. Parfitt et al., 'Vitamin D and Bone Health in the Elderly', *American Journal of Clinical Nutrition* 36, p.1014, 1982.

D.E.M. Lawson, 'Relative Contributions of Diet and Sunlight to Vitamin D State in the Elderly', *British Medical Journal* 2, pp.303-305, 1979.

M.E. Poskitt et al., 'Diet, Sunlight and 250HD in Healthy Children and Adults', *British Medical Journal* 1, pp.221-3, 1972.

N.E. Rosenthal et al., 'Seasonal Affective Disorder in Children and Adolescents', *American Journal of Psychiatry* 143, 3, pp.356-8, March 1986.

N.E. Rosenthal et al., 'Antidepressant Effects of Light in Seasonal Affective Disorder', *American Journal of Psychiatry* 142, pp.163-70, 1985.

J.J. Lopez-Ibor, 'The Involvement of Serotonin in Psychiatric Disorders and Behaviour', *British Journal of Psychiatry* 153, suppl. 3, pp.26-39, 1988.

B.T. Jones, R.H. Loiselle, 'Reversibility of Serotonin Irritation Syndrome with Atmospheric Anions' *Journal of Clinical Psychiatry* 47, pp.141-3, 1986.

E. Lester et al., 'Seasonal Variations in Serum 25-Hydroxyvitamin D in the Elderly in Britain', *Lancet* 2, pp.979-80, 1979.

Chapter 7

COUGHS, SNEEZES, AND WINTER DISEASES

It is not necessarily the drop in temperature that makes us more prone to infection in the winter. When the windows are closed and heating is used, the air becomes drier and the subsequent decrease in humidity increases the survival time of viruses and bacteria. Cross-infection is much more likely, especially in schools and the work-place, or anywhere people are in close contact with each other in a closed, heated, indoor environment.

Winter can also be a time of greater stress. Christmas shopping, cooking, and parties are one example, and the stress of being cold is another. We are all exposed to less fresh air and sunlight, and eat less fresh or raw fruit and vegetables during the winter. Other factors that decrease immune response, or lead to an increase in annoying ailments include: less exercise, and the more frequent use of over-the-counter or prescription medicines which may have side-effects or decrease nutrients (see Chapter 9).

There are many different natural remedies to help overcome winter infections and ailments. Use the suggestions in this chapter to help yourself, and your family, to a healthier winter.

ATHLETE'S FOOT/TINEA

Athlete's foot is a common winter complaint because millions of pairs of feet are confined to shoes, wellies, or plastic footwear during the cold weather. Athlete's foot is a fungal infection that loves warm, damp, dark places, and this is why it favours the crevices between the toes. It can be picked up very easily when walking bare-foot on floors around public swimming pools, showers, health clubs and saunas, and once acquired it may remain dormant until the right conditions prevail to activate it.

SELF-HELP ACTION PLAN

☑ Wash the feet once or twice daily in warm water to which 2 tablespoons of apple cider vinegar have been added. Use a mild, natural shampoo rather than soap. Pat the feet dry, taking care to dry in between the toes. Avoid rubbing the area as this activates the itching which accompanies athlete's foot.

☑ Whenever possible, wear only pure cotton socks and make sure that your footwear is made from a material that can 'breathe'. Try not to wear the same pair of shoes all day, every day. If your work compels you to wear nylon tights, then remove them as soon as you return home and wash your feet well.

☑ Use a personal bath mat, and a separate cloth for the area affected with athlete's foot. Wash all items that have been in contact with an affected area in hot water to kill the fungus.

☑ Wear protective footwear in public swimming pools, or health clubs.

NATURE'S MEDICINE CHEST

Treatment From The Inside, Out

☑ Try to include plenty of yogurt and some garlic in your diet. Cut down on sugar, sweets, and alcohol if you can.

☑ Ensure that your diet contains plenty of vitamins A, C, and B-complex, also manganese and zinc. Manganese can be found in many wholefoods, especially asparagus, oats, wheatgerm, avocados, nuts, rye bread, fruit, vegetables, and fish. For the other nutrients, see Chapter 3 for the Food Sources Quick Reference Chart.

☑ The homoeopathic tissue salt Kali sulph. may also be used safely by children or adults, to help athlete's foot.

External Remedies

✔ Apply undiluted pure tea tree oil to the area at least twice a day. If the skin has actually split between the toes the tea tree oil may sting slightly but this will stop after a few moments. This oil is harmless to skin, but is a natural antifungal agent that will kill the fungus and keep the infection in check. If the nails are also affected, tea tree oil can be applied 2-3 times a day. If you cannot obtain tea tree oil from your health food store, apply some uncooked honey to cotton wool and place this between the toes overnight, wearing some old cotton socks to protect the sheets.

✔ Green clay can be used as dusting powder because it is absorbent and healing. When sprinkled liberally over your feet and between the toes, green clay can help to counteract the effect of wearing nylon tights all day; but beware, it will stain clothing green. Golden seal root powder can also be used as a dusting powder; however, it is expensive and will permanently stain clothing bright yellow.

HELP YOURSELF — QUICK GUIDE

Wear protective footwear when walking around swimming pools, showers, saunas, health clubs, etc.

Wear cotton socks, and footwear which 'breathes'.

Use green clay as a dusting powder for the feet.

Ensure that socks and cloths that have been in contact with the infected area are washed in very hot water to kill the fungus.

Use your own bath mat to prevent spreading the infection to others.

Avoid wearing nylon socks, nylon tights, training shoes, gym shoes, or plastic shoes.

BAD CIRCULATION

The seasonal change is a difficult time for the body, as it has to adapt to the winter chill. Cold hands and feet develop very easily even in a warm room if circulation is sluggish, and this can increase susceptibility to problems such as chilblains, and even hypothermia. Circulation decreases when there is prolonged inactivity such as sitting for long periods of time, or being confined to bed. Getting muscles moving creates body heat, and acts as a pump to aid the heart in moving blood around the body, especially to the furthest regions such as arms and legs. When muscles are relaxed, the heart has to do all the work, and this may result in sluggish circulation to the extremities. One of the side-effects of beta blockers is cold hands and feet: see Chapter 9. If you are taking these drugs, do not increase your activity without consulting your doctor.

SELF-HELP ACTION PLAN

☑ Exercise is the prime remedy for bad circulation which is caused by tension and inactivity. It stimulates deep breathing, oxygen intake, and general circulation. Outdoor exercise in the fresh air is most effective, but indoor exercise with the window open is also beneficial in extremely bad weather. For winter exercise ideas see Chapter 5.

☑ Hot and cold water may be used to increase circulation, especially to the hands or feet. Half fill a bowl or bucket with medium hot water, and another with cold water. Immerse the feet or hands first in the hot water for 2-3 minutes, then in the cold for approximately 10 seconds. Repeat about five times. Towel dry, and massage feet with oil.

☑ Circulation is stimulated by using a loofah when showering or bathing, and by vigorously towelling yourself dry. An alternative is to use a vegetable fibre skin brush (not nylon as it may damage the skin) to increase circulation, stimulate the skin's ability to eliminate toxins, and remove dead skin cells. Lay a towel on the floor, stand in the middle, and start brushing at the feet and progress upwards, using the brush in a circular motion, towards the heart. Avoid brushing the breasts, face and neck. When you have finished brushing, take the towel and brush outside and remove the dead skin cells from them by shaking the towel, and brushing the bristles of the skinbrush with your hand. It is very important to do this outside, otherwise the dead skin cells will create more dust in the home. Vegetable fibre brushes can be obtained in some health foods stores, or if you have difficulty finding one, see Chapter 11.

☑ Avoid wearing girdles, and waistbands, socks, or underwear with tight elastic; these can all decrease circulation and lead to cold extremities. Girdles and tight waistbands also restrict the diaphragm, which causes shallow breathing and leads to bad circulation.

☑ Smoking cigarettes and other tobacco products causes constriction of the arteries, veins and capillaries, and can cut down circulation to all parts of the body.

HELP YOURSELF — QUICK GUIDE

Take plenty of exercise in the fresh air.

Use a loofah or skin brush to stimulate circulation.

Get up and move regularly if you spend a considerable amount of time sitting.

Avoid tight clothing as it restricts circulation and breathing.

Always exercise in the fresh air whenever possible.

CATARRH

Mucus is one of the body's first lines of defence against infectious micro-organisms, pollutants, and irritants. It protects the mucous membranes that line the respiratory, digestive, reproductive, and urinary systems. If the mucous membranes become inflamed or irritated, then the production of mucus is increased. When excessive amounts are produced, this sticky discharge becomes known as catarrh. The congested feeling in the head that may accompany colds or flu is caused by a build-up of catarrh in the sinuses.

SELF-HELP ACTION PLAN

Excessive quantities of mucus are usually produced by the body in order to discharge infectious or irritating substances. If you are suffering from catarrh, it is important to consult your doctor in order to find out whether you have an infection, or serious congestion of the lungs. There are various other possible causes of catarrh: tobacco smoke, pollution, dietary choices, heated indoor environments, and allergens are probably the most common.

- Always blow your nose by clearing one nostril at a time. Keep one side closed by pressing on it. Avoid pressing on both nostrils at once because as you blow, mucus will be forced into the ear's Eustachian tube and may spread infection to the ear. It may also force air into the middle ear and rupture the ear drum.

- Stale, dry, heated air and irritants such as pollution and tobacco smoke can trigger catarrh. Research indicates that these conditions slow the beat of tiny hairs lining the airways. These hairs, known as cilia, are the road-sweepers of the respiratory system, but when their work is hindered, mucus and other material may begin to accumulate, leading to congestion. Opening windows changes and clears the air, but if this is not possible, an ionizer can help. Negative ions produced by the unit clean and freshen the air, and for some people an ionizer can help alleviate winter catarrhal miseries. It may also help to use a vaporizer as moist air liquefies secretions and makes it easier for cilia to discharge them.

- If you use a nasal decongestant spray regularly, this may be making your congestion worse. Decongestant preparations should only be used in the recommended doses, up to three days at a time, in order to prevent a rebound effect occurring which causes blocked breathing passages.

Nasal decongestants work by shrinking blood vessels in the nose and opening the airways, but using them for several days causes the blood vessels to swell, and more mucus to be produced, which blocks breathing and can eventually damage and scar nasal tissues.

Decongestants should not be used by people with high blood pressure, diabetes, heart disease, or thyroid disease. Consult your doctor for advice if you have found that you need to use one of these sprays regularly. While you are gradually discontinuing its use, try the steam inhalation method outlined below

☑ An overall look at diet and lifestyle may be needed to pinpoint the reason for catarrhal congestion, and a natural practitioner can help. See Finding a Natural Practitioner in Chapter 11.

NATURE'S MEDICINE CHEST

☑ Steam inhalation helps to loosen and discharge tenacious catarrh in the nasal passages and lungs. It can also be used during bouts of laryngitis. Fill a saucepan or non-plastic bowl with boiling water and add a little peppermint, eucalyptus, Olbas oil, or friar's balsam. Drape a large towel over your head and lean over the bowl from a height of about 12 inches (30cm). Be very careful not to burn yourself in the hot steam. Breathe in the steam for about five minutes, and blow your nose gently afterwards, following the method outlined on page 131. Try this once or twice a day for up to ten days. Alternatively, to help night-time congestion, put a little Olbas oil on a handkerchief and place it on your pillow.

☑ Dietary choices that may stimulate the production of mucus include an over-reliance on processed and refined carbohydrates. White bread, cakes, biscuits, and sweets made from white sugar and flour fall into this category. For some people a high intake of dairy products such as cow's milk, cheese, cream, butter; fried foods; and cocoa or chocolate can contribute to catarrhal congestion. The diet should include plenty of wholefoods, and potassium-rich fresh fruit and vegetables.

✔ If you own a vegetable juicer, drink a daily glass of fresh juice made from a combination of carrots, a clove of garlic, cucumber, and celery.

✔ Vegetables and herbs which cause the eyes and nose to run are nature's remedy for catarrh. Try adding Japanese daikon radish, a little grated horseradish, crushed garlic, onions, watercress, and nasturtium leaves to your daily salad. These vegetables and herbs have strong antiseptic qualities and because they are high in sulphur, together with other minerals including germanium, they are very effective anti-catarrhal, and anti-infective agents. If you are unable to tolerate crushed garlic, try taking one garlic capsule three times a day, saving the last one to be taken after your last meal of the day.

✔ There are numerous herbal remedies for catarrh. These include couch grass which is used at the early stages of catarrh; cornsilk for obstinate cases; and coltsfoot for loosening catarrh in the airways. A herbal nightcap to ease suffocating catarrh can be made by pouring boiling water over the following herbs in a non-metal teapot: half a teaspoon of slippery elm powder, half a teaspoon of crushed fenugreek seeds, half a teaspoon of mullein leaves, half a teaspoon of lemon balm leaves. Allow to steep for up to five minutes; then strain into a cup, add a little honey and a squeeze of fresh lemon juice. Sip slowly. Prop yourself up with an extra pillow, as this will also make it easier to breathe.

✔ For sinus congestion caused by infection, crush a clove of garlic into half a cup of previously boiled, blood-heat spring water. Using an eye dropper, draw up some liquid, lie back and hold your breath, then place ten drops into each nostril. Repeat this procedure three times a day for three days.

✔ General homoeopathic remedies for catarrhal conditions include: Thuja, Kali bich., Euphrasia. Hydrastis for post-nasal drip and deafness. Kali bich. for white and stringy mucous. Tissue salts include: Ferr. phos. for the first stages of congestion; Kali mur. when there is thick white phlegm and stuffiness; Nat. mur. for watery catarrh with loss of the sense of taste and smell. New Era combination Q is for catarrh and sinus congestion. The remedies can be used safely by adults or children.

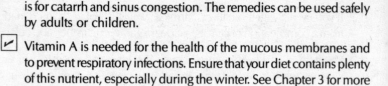 Vitamin A is needed for the health of the mucous membranes and to prevent respiratory infections. Ensure that your diet contains plenty of this nutrient, especially during the winter. See Chapter 3 for more information.

Royal jelly and vitamin C both support adrenal gland function and, like exercise, encourage the production of adrenaline which is naturally decongestant.

HELP YOURSELF — QUICK GUIDE

Check with your doctor if the catarrhal condition is chronic or distressing.

Seek help from a natural practitioner in order to find the underlying cause of the catarrh.

Try to avoid smoking and smoky atmospheres.

Ensure that there is adequate humidity in heated rooms.

Include plenty of vitamin A in your diet.

For severe night congestion, sleep with two or more pillows to raise your head.

Nasal decongestant sprays should not be used for longer than three days, to prevent worsening of the congestion.

Avoid too many milk products and white flour or sugar.

CHAPPED AND CRACKED SKIN

Cold windy weather and heating are the two main causes of this often painful complaint, and people who are prone to dry skin are likely to suffer the most during the winter. Frigid air, and the ill-effects of indoor heating, can cause drying that goes deeper and is potentially more damaging than summer heat.

SELF-HELP ACTION PLAN

✔ If your favourite winter sport is sitting in front of a blazing fire, your skin could be suffering. Protect it with a moisturizing gel if you have oily skin, or a good moisturizing cream if you have normal to dry skin. Always protect your skin from cold and wind, they can both cause drying and damage. Once a week treat your face to a moisturizing facial pack made by mixing a teaspoon of brewer's yeast with a mashed ripe avocado, and the contents of a vitamin E capsule.

✔ Low humidity in heated rooms causes the skin to lose moisture, and this can be counteracted by placing a bowl of water close to the fireplace, or on central heating radiators; an alternative is to use a room humidifier.

NATURE'S MEDICINE CHEST

External Remedies

✔ If you suffer from cracks on the palms of your hands or on fingers and thumbs, always wear rubber gloves when washing dishes, and dry your hands well. Use a moisturizing cream which contains herbs such as calendula (marigold) or comfrey, and always wear gloves in very cold weather. See Treatment From the Inside, Out, in this section for information about important nutrients.

✔ To soften and heal chapped hands make a paste from finely ground oatmeal and water with a little aloe juice added. Calendula cream or ointment will help to heal cracked skin, as will aloe gel. Creams containing bee pollen and honey help cracked and peeling skin.

Treatment From the Inside, Out

✔ If you suffer from cracks in the fingers, a regular dose of emulsified cod liver oil may help, or include a capsule of vitamin A and D with any meal of the day which includes vegetable oil or other fats.

✔ Cracks in the corners of the lips are often helped by increasing the intake of vitamins B2, B12, zinc, and vitamin A. A high potency multiple vitamin/mineral tablet taken once a day, with the addition of an extra 25mg of B2 with breakfast and lunch, should help. Continue using the extra B2 until the cracks have healed. It may also be necessary to increase your intake of vitamins A and D by taking some emulsified cod liver oil or vitamin A and D capsules for up to a week.

Vegetarians and vegans may be particularly susceptible to cracks and splits around the lips, and this may become a problem particularly in the winter, and after 3-5 years have elapsed after changing to a diet free of animal products. The cracks may be the symptom of a vitamin B12 deficiency; for more information see B12 in the Immune Nutrients Quick Reference Chart in Chapter 3.

✔ Ensure that your diet contains plenty of vitamin C, because it encourages healing and collagen formation; vitamins A and D, which are vital for skin health; and vitamin E and zinc, which encourage and speed healing. For good sources of vitamins and minerals see Chapter 3.

✔ The homoeopathic tissue salt Calc. fluor. is for chapped and cracked skin.

HELP YOURSELF — QUICK GUIDE

Ensure that you have plenty of vitamins C, A, and D in your diet, and if the skin complaint is particularly bad, try taking emulsified cod liver oil every day.

Always wear gloves when washing dishes, and when going out in cold weather.

Use a good moisturizer on your skin during the winter.

Cracks around the mouth can be helped with B2, A, and zinc.

A vaporizer will help to keep skin supple in dry atmospheres.

CHILBLAINS

Chilblains are small red or purple patches which may appear on the toes, heels, and fingers in cold, damp weather. They are caused by congestion and swelling of the skin and may begin by itching, but become very painful. Children seem to be particularly susceptible to this disorder, and women seem to be more affected than men.

SELF-HELP ACTION PLAN

- Chilblains can be prevented by keeping the circulation moving, and the feet warm. When bathing use a loofah or circulation mit, and towel yourself dry vigorously.

- When entering the house after exposure to cold and damp, resist the temptation to put your icy hands or feet on the radiator or in front of the fire. Instead, encourage the circulation by rubbing your hands together and massaging the feet. When you feel warmer put on thick, dry cotton socks, and slippers.

- Avoid wearing tight gloves, socks, and shoes. Use mittens instead of gloves.

- Exercise is very important as it keeps the circulation moving and warms the extremities. Remember, it is the movement of muscles which creates heat. See Chapter 1 for more information about body heat.

- Smoking should be avoided because nicotine directly cuts down circulation to the extremities.

NATURE'S MEDICINE CHEST

External Remedies

✓ There are numerous natural remedies which work to heal chilblains. If the skin is unbroken, gently rub lemon juice or witch hazel into the skin and when it dries, massage the feet well with olive oil.

✓ Soothing and healing applications include Nelson's homoeopathic cream for chilblains, comfrey ointment, calendula cream, and aloe vera.

✓ See Bad Circulation in this chapter for ways of using water to increase circulation and ease chilblains.

Treatment From the Inside, Out

✓ The tissue salts Calc. phos., Kali phos., and New Era combination P are used for chilblains, and are safe for both adults and children.

✓ Eat a variety of whole foods and plenty of fresh fruit and vegetables. The diet should contain foods rich in calcium and magnesium, vitamins C, E, and B-complex. For information on vitamins and minerals, see Food Sources Quick Reference Chart in Chapter 3.

NOTE: Vitamin B3 helps circulation, but it also causes the blood vessels to open, causing a rapid loss of heat from the body. If the weather or your home is very cold, avoid using doses of niacin or nicotinamide over 50mg, and concentrate instead on B3-rich foods such as brewer's yeast, eggs, fish, green leafy vegetables, beans and peas, liver, sunflower seeds, and wheatgerm.

✓ Vitamin C and rutin can be taken in supplement form to help healing and circulation.

HELP YOURSELF — QUICK GUIDE

Keep the feet and hands warm in the winter, and keep the circulation moving.

Eat a variety of wholefoods and fresh fruit and vegetables.

Avoid the temptation to put freezing cold hands and feet on hot radiators, hot water bottles, or in front of the fire.

Tight or restrictive clothing will make you feel colder by decreasing circulation.

Smoking cuts down circulation to the extremities.

COLDS AND FLU

Every year new strains of influenza develop, and although the immune system has blueprints for antibodies against the types of flu that it has already been exposed to, it does not have antibodies to deal with new strains. Because viruses have the ability to change, it gives them an advantage over a weakened immune system, which is why so many people are particularly vulnerable to infections during the winter. Micro-organisms are spread by the water droplets in the air from sneezing and coughing, and also through hand contact, or contact with items that have been touched by someone with an infection. Coughs cause air to be released from the lungs at speeds approaching 60mph, enough to traject infectious micro-organisms several yards through the air. The first signs of flu include a temperature rise to 101°F (38.3°C), chills, headache, muscle and/or backache, and extreme tiredness.

SELF-HELP ACTION PLAN

✔ At the first signs of a cold or flu it is important to keep the body warm and go to bed as early as possible. If you have a fever, go to bed, keep the covers around you, and relax. The air in your room should not be dry. Drink plenty of hot mineral water with a squeeze of fresh lemon juice. Avoid taking aspirin or paracetamol immediately a fever develops. Aspirin reduces the body's vitamin C and may make a cold worse by increasing the virus and lowering the immune response. If aspirin is taken with alcohol, or a cold remedy that contains it, the chance of the side-effect of stomach bleeding will be greater.

In adults, a temperature of 100–102°F should be allowed to run its course, because elevated body temperature helps to kill viruses and other micro-organisms. A doctor must be consulted, however, if the temperature remains raised to 102°F or greater, causes severe discomfort, or lasts longer than three days. Feverfew can be used to bring a fever down, but should be avoided if you are taking the contraceptive pill because it can increase the chance of breakthrough bleeding and pregnancy.

Never give aspirin, or aspirin-based medicines, to children under 12 except under medical supervision. This precaution has been recommended by the Committee on Safety of Medicines because of aspirin's link with Reye's syndrome, a rare but potentially lethal childhood illness which can damage the brain and liver. If aspirin is given to a child infected with chickenpox or flu, the danger of developing Reye's syndrome is further increased. See Chapter 1 for more information on fever and body heat.

Eating sweet foods and sugar at the onset of a cold or infection decreases the number of active lymphocytes in the immune system. To help your body fight an infection, avoid sugar in all forms for at least the first three days.

NATURE'S MEDICINE CHEST

If natural remedies do not seem to help after two days, and the infection goes to the chest, contact your doctor for advice.

☑ To increase your immune system's infection-fighting power, abstain from food for the first day and a half of an infection. Drink plenty of fresh vegetable juices, rosehip or chamomile tea, and hot mineral water with a squeeze of fresh lemon juice and a little freshly grated ginger root. After 48 hours foods should be resumed, but the meals should be light, with the emphasis on vegetables and easily digested proteins such as fish. During an infection it is important to maintain your intake of amino acids, because these components of protein are involved in the manufacture and maintenance of white blood cells. If your protein intake is low, it may be necessary to take an amino acid complex supplement for seven to ten days.

☑ Langdale's cinnamon essence can be taken to help fight colds and flu as it provides the antiseptic benefits of cinnamon. Children over 5 can be given half a teaspoonful of cinnamon essence in warm water up to three times a day, and adults, one teaspoonful three times a day.

☑ Many adults find that taking vitamin C and bioflavonoids helps the body overcome colds and flu. In order to be really effective, Vitamin C often needs to be taken in very large doses, sometimes up to 1000mg six to ten times a day. This dosage may need to be maintained for up to three days, and then gradually reduced over the next seven to ten days. Ensure that your diet contains foods rich in calcium and magnesium and vitamin B12 when using high doses of vitamin C.

IMPORTANT: See Checklist 3 to make sure that a high intake of vitamin C will not interfere with any medicine you may be taking.

☑ Babies and children may be given frequent small doses of warm, diluted chamomile tea. Chamomile is soothing and anti-infective.

☑ A pungent, adult flu remedy can be made by adding the following ingredients to 8 fl. oz (225ml) of organic cider vinegar:

⅛ teaspoon cayenne pepper
2 crushed garlic cloves
1 oz (28g) grated fresh ginger root.

Add one tablespoon of the mixture to a cup of warm water, and drink approximately every two hours. If you have a hiatus hernia, or stomach ulcer, avoid using this remedy as it can irritate these conditions.

✔ Thyme tea can be used by adults for its antiseptic qualities. Make the tea in a thermos flask to prevent the pungent oils from evaporating into the air. Put 1 teaspoon thyme, ⅛ teaspoon of cayenne pepper, and 1 teaspoon of peppermint into the flask and add a pint of boiling filtered or spring water. Allow to steep for ten minutes, then strain and return to the flask. Pour out a cupful and sip slowly. Use three cups per day.

✔ Homoeopathic remedies may be used by adults and children. Aconite is indicated when symptoms such as high fever, thirst, restlessness, and sensitivity to light come on suddenly, but it should only be taken for the first 24 hours of the infection. Gelsemium is used for influenza when there are shivers up and down the spine, aches in the limbs and back, tight-feeling headache, and lack of thirst even with fever. Belladonna is indicated when there is a sudden onset of high fever with flushed face and racing pulse, and a pounding in the head. Please note that homoeopathic medicines may be counteracted if taken with cinnamon essence, or any remedies which contain pungent oils such as peppermint or thyme.

✔ During fever a large quantity of fluid is lost in perspiration, so it is vital to keep drinking even if you do not feel thirsty. Hot mineral water and lemon juice will supply much-needed fluid, minerals and vitamin C. Other drinks can include rosehip, elderflower, chamomile or yarrow teas; fresh vegetable juices, especially a mixture of carrot, beet, and celery with a quarter of a clove of garlic; and green juices such as wheat or barley grass juice. See wheatgrass under Indoor Gardening in Chapter 3.

✔ Minerals are lost during a fever and need to be replaced through the diet, but if you do not feel like eating there is a danger of mineral deficiencies developing. Children and the elderly are particularly vulnerable, and anyone using diuretics is also at particular risk. To remedy this, use the following simple recipe to make a mineral-rich vegetable soup or broth:

2 pints of spring or filtered water
Vecon vegetable stock
2 carrots
1 large leek
1 medium onion
2 cloves of garlic, crushed
2 large organically grown potatoes
1 parsnip
1 turnip

Wash and chop the vegetables. The potatoes should be cut in half to reveal a light ring about ½ in (1cm) below the skin. The highest concentration of minerals, especially potassium, lie within the first half inch, and the starchy interior of the potato should be discarded. Put the chopped vegetables in a non-aluminium saucepan and add the water and seasoning. Bring to the boil and simmer for approximately half an hour, or until all the vegetables are tender. The soup can now be served, or mixed in a blender to make it thick. If you do not feel like eating, strain off some broth and sip it slowly. Sprinkle a little freshly chopped parsley into each serving.

Alternatively use 8-16 fl. oz. (225-450ml) of fresh vegetable juices every day, and for up to five days after the fever has passed. A combination of carrot, celery, beet, cucumber, half a clove of garlic, and 2-3 sprigs of parsley will provide easily absorbed minerals and vitamins.

✔ Supplements of vitamins and minerals may be taken when a fever has passed. An adult supplement regime for a week could include up to 10,000iu of vitamin A per day, a teaspoon of *Bio Strath* three times a day or 25mg of B-complex twice a day, and two daily multi-mineral tablets.

✔ Royal jelly is a naturally rich source of pantothenic acid or B5, and this is important for adrenal function in tandem with vitamin C. See Chapter 2 for information about the involvement of vitamin C in maintaining a healthy immune system.

HELP YOURSELF — QUICK GUIDE

In adults, allow a fever to run its course unless it reaches more than 102°F, causes severe discomfort, or lasts for more than three days.

At the very first signs of an infection, keep warm and drink plenty of hot mineral water with fresh lemon juice.

Avoid sugar in all forms at the first signs of, and during, an infection.

Don't take aspirin or paracetamol unless it is absolutely necessary to bring a fever down.

Aspirin should never be given to children under 12.

COLD SORES

Cold sores on the lips, mouth, and rim of the nose arise from the herpes simplex 1 virus, which is often acquired during childhood, and through contact with an infected person. The virus remains dormant in nerve tissue until activated. The immune system keeps the virus in check but fever, illness, stress, or even food allergies can lower the immune response enough for the virus to become active. Some women find that they are particularly vulnerable just before their periods, and blisters frequently appear after excessive exposure to strong sunlight. The first sign of a developing blister is itching in the infected area followed by redness, and then swelling and crustiness. When the blisters are moist they are infectious, and although this complaint is not dangerous, the blisters can be embarrassingly unsightly, and produce misery well out of proportion to their size.

NATURE'S MEDICINE CHEST

External Remedies

☑ At the first tingle of a developing blister, apply pure tea tree oil directly to the area, then every hour through the day. This antiseptic oil can reduce pain and itching and seems to shorten the severity and duration of the sore.

☑ Another way to stop a developing blister in its tracks is to apply ice to the area immediately any itching or tingling is felt.

☑ Aloe vera gel can be applied to blisters to help healing and prevent scarring. Vitamin E can also be applied directly to the blisters three times a day.

☑ Tincture of lavender or diluted tincture of myrrh can be applied to the sore. They are both antiseptic and soothing.

☑ Some people have found that applying a paste made from instant coffee and water can stop a developing blister.

Treatment From the Inside, Out

☑ Prevention is better than cure, because once a herpes blister has begun to develop, remedies of all kinds rarely stop it from running its course, and, at best, only decrease the severity and duration of the sore. Preventive measures include getting plenty of anti-viral vitamins A and C, and bioflavonoids in the diet. Many people find that the virus is more active in the winter, and one reason may be that the liver is reluctant to give up its stores of vitamin A as the weather gets colder. Ensuring that the diet contains enough vitamin A and zinc will help to counteract this. Often, poor absorption of calcium and magnesium and a low intake of fatty acids contribute to the outbreak of cold sores.

A vitamin/mineral supplement regime could include 250mg of vitamin C and bioflavonoids twice a day, B-complex 25mg twice a day, at least 2,500mg of vitamin A once a day, and calcium and magnesium after the evening meal. For more information on the immune system see Chapters 2 and 3.

✔ Strict vegetarians or vegans may suffer from frequent outbreaks of cold sores because the dietary intake of vitamin B12 may not be adequate. See Chapter 3 for dietary sources.

✔ Vegetarian or vegan diets may also be high in the amino acid arginine, and this appears to encourage the virus. Arginine is abundant in almonds, cashews, carob, chocolate, oats, peanuts, pecans, seeds, wholewheat and white flour, cereals, and wheatgerm. The amino acid L-lysine discourages the virus, so lysine-rich foods should also be eaten to create a balance. Lysine is found in beans, beef, brewer's yeast, cheese, chicken, fish, lamb, milk, mung sprouts, and most fruit and vegetables. If the outbreaks of cold sores are extremely frequent it will be necessary to take steps to boost the function of the immune system; see Chapters 2 and 3. For vegans it may help to take a daily supplement of up to 250mg of L-lysine to help balance the intake of lysine and arginine.

✔ Keeping the intestinal bacteria healthy aids immune function and helps the body to keep the herpes virus in check. Eat plenty of 'live' yogurt, and if necessary supplement the diet with acidophilus powder or capsules. *Molkosan*, a concentrated liquid whey from milk, also helps to encourage healthy bacteria to thrive. A regular daily intake is often all that is needed to prevent herpes recurring.

✔ Try adding a teaspoon of virgin, cold-pressed olive oil to your daily salad for protection against the herpes virus.

✔ Avoid drinking coffee and alcohol as they both increase your need for vitamins A, C, and B complex, as well as zinc.

✔ Decrease your intake of refined sugar and white flour, and restrict citrus fruits, but do eat plenty of other fresh fruit and vegetables.

HELP YOURSELF — QUICK GUIDE

Include plenty of vitamin A, C, and B-complex in the diet, especially if you have a cold or are under stress.

Drink some *Molkosan* whey concentrate every day, as a preventative.

Apply pure tea tree oil, or ice, at the first sign of a developing blister.

Avoid a diet high in arginine.

Try not to rub or bite the lips as this may sometimes activate the virus.

Avoid drinking too much coffee or alcohol.

COUGHS AND CHESTINESS

The lungs are especially at risk from infection in the winter because the common cold virus can spread down the airways, causing inflammation which may lead to acute bronchitis. People who have asthma, smokers, and those who live in areas with high atmospheric pollution are the most susceptible to bronchitis and chest infections. Respiratory tract infections tend to be more common during childhood than at any other time, but the elderly living in poor housing conditions also suffer from frequent respiratory complaints during the winter.

An acute cough is a necessary evil, because it clears blocked breathing passages in a natural attempt to remove phlegm and irritants from the airways. Any attempt to suppress an acute cough can make an infection worse because mucus and infectious micro-organisms are retained. Smokers are more prone to serious respiratory infections because they are less able to cough up bronchial catarrh and clear infected bronchial tubes.

Any infection that settles on the chest should be reported to a doctor immediately, especially if the attacks are repeated. For occasional, mild coughs and chestiness, natural remedies may be used, but if no relief is obtained within two days, or the infection worsens with an increase in thick green phlegm, it is important to contact your doctor for advice, as it may be dangerous not to seek medical help. Also contact your doctor if there is shortness of breath, difficulty in breathing, severe cough in a young child, increased temperature with cough, any signs of blood when coughing, or a pain in the chest when breathing.

SELF-HELP ACTION PLAN

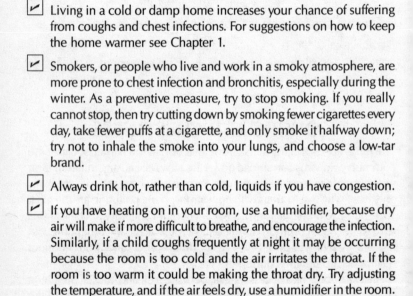

☑ Living in a cold or damp home increases your chance of suffering from coughs and chest infections. For suggestions on how to keep the home warmer see Chapter 1.

☑ Smokers, or people who live and work in a smoky atmosphere, are more prone to chest infection and bronchitis, especially during the winter. As a preventive measure, try to stop smoking. If you really cannot stop, then try cutting down by smoking fewer cigarettes every day, take fewer puffs at a cigarette, and only smoke it halfway down; try not to inhale the smoke into your lungs, and choose a low-tar brand.

☑ Always drink hot, rather than cold, liquids if you have congestion.

☑ If you have heating on in your room, use a humidifier, because dry air will make if more difficult to breathe, and encourage the infection. Similarly, if a child coughs frequently at night it may be occurring because the room is too cold and the air irritates the throat. If the room is too warm it could be making the throat dry. Try adjusting the temperature, and if the air feels dry, use a humidifier in the room. Contact your doctor if the cough persists.

☑ If you are normally in good health and do not suffer from severe breathing disorders, you can use the following method to help loosen bronchial catarrh. Breathe in, and place your hands over your ribs. Move them up and down rapidly for about 30 seconds, in order to create a vibration in the chest which will loosen catarrh. Cough once or twice, deeply from the bottom of the chest.

✓ Breathing difficulties can cause panic which creates tension and makes it harder to breathe. Try to stay as relaxed as possible; it will help breathing. If you have any difficulty breathing, contact your doctor immediately.

✓ Always breathe through your nose as it acts as a filter, and use a mask when working in dusty areas.

✓ Practise deep breathing. Use your diaphragm and stomach muscles while keeping your upper chest relaxed.

NATURE'S MEDICINE CHEST

Natural remedies can be used to help occasional bouts of chestiness and coughs. Most of the remedies loosen, and help to excrete mucus and are classed as expectorants. For other related information see Colds and Catarrh in this chapter.

Children's Cough Tea

Mix the following herbs together in a clean, dry container:

½ oz (14g) thyme
1 oz mullein leaves
1 oz plaintain

Put a ¼ teaspoon of the herb mixture in a non-metal teapot. Pour boiling filtered water over the herbs and allow to steep for three minutes. Strain, and use when lukewarm. Use two to four cups per day.

Children's Sore Throat, Cough and Respiratory Tea

Chamomile is very soothing, and has mild antiseptic qualities, which is why it often helps mild throat and respiratory complaints. Put ½ teaspoon of German chamomile flowers into a non-metallic teapot. Pour a cup of boiling water over the herbs and steep for three minutes. Strain, then use when warm. Up to three cups may be taken each day.

Herbal Cough Remedy

This remedy may be used by adults, and children over 12.

Mix the following herbs together in a clean, dry container:
1 oz (28g) slippery elm powder
1 oz thyme
1 oz licorice
1 oz crushed fennel seeds or fennel powder

Put ½ teaspoon of the mixed herbs in a non-metallic teapot, add boiling water and steep for three minutes. Strain and sip the hot tea slowly. Use up to three cups per day. NOTE: If you are prone to breast tenderness avoid large quantities of licorice; also, if you are taking antihypertensive medicines, calcium antagonists, diuretics, or other medicines for high blood pressure, avoid licorice as it can cause salt and water retention and may decrease the effects of the drugs.

Elderberry Syrup for Chesty Colds
For adults and children over 12. To make elderberry syrup bring to the boil 4lb (approx. 2kg) of fresh, ripe, crushed elderberries with 1lb (½kg) of honey or 16 fl oz (1¾l) of concentrated fruit juice. Simmer for 30 minutes, strain, then evaporate the juice to the thickness of the syrup. Transfer to sterilized glass bottles, and store for the winter. Add 2 tablespoonsful to a cup of hot water at bedtime to help relieve chestiness and induce perspiration.

Herbal Help for Smoker's Cough
Mix the following herbs together in a clean, dry container:

1 oz (28g) hyssop
1 oz black horehound
1 oz coltsfoot
1 oz marshmallow root
1 oz licorice

Place ½ teaspoon of the mixture in a non-metallic teapot and pour boiling water over it. Allow to steep for three minutes, then strain and drink. Up to three cups a day may be taken. See the information about licorice under Cough Remedy in this section.

Horehound Cough Drops

For adults and children over 12: add 2 oz (55g) dry horehound leaves to 1 pint (1¾l) spring or filtered water. Boil for ten minutes, then allow to cool. Strain, then put it in a small saucepan and combine with 1lb (approx. ½kg) honey and ⅛ teaspoon cream of tartar. Stir until honey is dissolved, then cook over a low heat until a little of the mixture becomes a hard ball when dropped in cold water. Drop about half a teaspoon at a time into the water, until you have emptied the saucepan. When the drops have dried, roll them in a little rice flour to prevent them from sticking to each other. Store the balls in a sterilized jar, and use up to six a day for up to a week.

Treatment From the Inside, Out

✔ Homoeopathic remedies for breathing difficulties include ipecacuanha used for rattling mucus, and inflamed bronchial tubes; bryonia for breathing difficulties with dry throat and chesty cough, huge thirst, and feeling worse when moving; Arsen. alb. for when, in order to draw breath, it helps to sit up or bend forward; pulsatilla for a dry cough, especially when lying down at night; and spongia for a dry barking cough. The tissue salt Ferr. phos. is used for acute, painful and irritating cough. Children and adults may use homoeopathic remedies safely.

✔ In order to minimize mucus production, it helps to exclude dairy products, sugar and refined carbohydrates. For more information, see Colds, and Catarrh in this chapter.

✔ See the Food Sources Quick Reference Chart in Chapter 2 to ensure that you are getting plenty of vitamins A, B, C, and E, and zinc. Vitamin A is especially important for the health of the respiratory system, and it is also anti-viral. To help the body overcome a cough or chest infection, it may be necessary to take some emulsified cod liver oil for 10-14 days, but if the thought of it revolts you, then take it in capsule form.

Vitamin C also has strong anti-viral properties and it may be used in supplement form. It is always better to take frequent, small doses of vitamin C and bioflavonoids rather than one large daily dose. Use 250mg of calcium, or sodium ascorbate powder, approximately every hour until the infection has subsided, then gradually reduce the amount of vitamin C over the next two weeks. Children will also benefit from extra vitamins A and C, but it is important to follow the dosage instructions on the products. If you are taking any medicines, see Checklist 3 at the end of this chapter, for information about medicine's interactions with vitamin C.

HELP YOURSELF — QUICK GUIDE

Avoid smoking, and smoky rooms.

Make sure that there is enough humidity in heated rooms.

Suck a zinc gluconate tablet at the first sign of a sore throat.

Get plenty of vitamins A, D, and C in your diet. You may need to take emulsified cod liver oil, to top up your intake of A and D.

Avoid sugar, refined carbohydrates, and milk products while you have a sore throat or infection.

CYSTITIS

Cystitis is one of the most commonly reported urinary tract infections, especially among women, although some men may also suffer from it. The main symptoms tend to be frequent and burning urination accompanied by pain in the abdomen. If the cystitis is severe there may be blood in the urine, back pain, alternating chills and fever, and general tiredness and aches.

One of the main causes of this disorder is the transference of *Escherichia coli* bacteria from the anal area to the bladder via the urethra. This can happen during sexual intercourse, when inserting tampons, or after using the lavatory. Other causes include the use of oral contraceptives, stress, shock, or using public swimming pools. Pressure on the bladder, caused by the womb or bladder being out of place, enables urine to collect in constricted areas and the resulting increase in bacteria may lead to pain and infection.

Usually the body's immune system protects against infection but when it is taxed due to poor diet or a stressful lifestyle, and if the vaginal pH is altered, then cystitis can develop. For most people, using relaxation and stress control techniques with dietary measures can help to reduce the recurrence of cystitis, but these should only be tried when your doctor has ruled out any serious medical reasons for the disorder.

SELF-HELP ACTION PLAN

☑ Wearing cotton underwear allows the skin to breathe and absorbs moisture, and this discourages infection. It is also important to keep your back warm.

☑ When washing the genital area use a gentle pH balanced cleanser such as a natural baby shampoo, and avoid soap because it is alkaline and can be irritating. Wash from front to back.

☑ It is better to use sanitary towels than tampons, and avoid long, hot soaks in the bath. Exercise, fresh air, and good posture are all helpful.

NATURE'S MEDICINE CHEST

Local Remedy

☑ An effective and safe vaginal douche can be made from natural ingredients. Plain 'live' yogurt helps to restore the vaginal pH balance and feeds healthy bacteria. Raw honey has anti-bacterial properties, and aloe vera possesses both anti-fungal and anti-bacterial qualities.

Mix together:
1 ounce plain, live yogurt
1 teaspoon raw, uncooked honey
1 tablespoon aloe vera gel or juice

This should be made daily and used once a day for up to a week, and then once a week for several weeks thereafter. Douche syringes and instructions for use are available from chemists.

Treatment From the Inside, Out

Sometimes prolonged use of the broad-spectrum antibiotics which are often prescribed for bladder infections may result in their recurrence. This is because antibiotics can cause secondary infections by decreasing the population of important intestinal bacteria which keep yeast infections under control.

If you do suffer from recurring cystitis then you may have a yeast infection and this should be discussed with your doctor. For more information about yeast infection, see also *The Pill Protection Plan* (Thorsons, 1989).

✔ If you are prone to cystitis, try to avoid a diet high in refined foods, sugar, salt, coffee, tea, alcohol, chocolate, and spices. Citrus fruit juices also aggravate the condition but unsweetened cranberry and cherry juice is often beneficial. It is best to avoid chlorinated and carbonated water, but plenty of spring or filtered water should be consumed during acute cystitis.

✔ Smoking should be stopped, or at least reduced. For help with reducing smoking, see Coughs and Chestiness in this chapter, and Chapter 11 under Smoking.

✔ Herbal tea to help cystitis can be made from ½ teaspoon each of buchu and uva ursi. Place the herbs in a teapot, pour boiling water over them and allow to steep for two or three minutes. A cup can be taken once or twice a day for up to a week.

To make an infusion of shave grass, boil a cup of water in a saucepan, remove it from the heat and add a teaspoon of the herb. Allow to steep for half an hour and drink one cup a day for up to a week. Do not exceed the suggested quantities unless under the direction of a herbalist.

✔ Supplements of vitamin C are important but should not exceed 200mg twice a day if the contraceptive pill is being taken.

Vitamin A is also very important and although supplements should be avoided if you are taking the Pill the diet should contain plenty of this nutrient. Significant dietary sources of vitamin A include dairy products, fatty fish, liver, dark green leafy vegetables and fruit, with the exception of citrus. Yeast-free vitamin B-complex and calcium and magnesium supplements can be an important part of a vitamin regime along with raw garlic or garlic capsules, and bee propolis. Both garlic and propolis have anti-infective qualities.

HELP YOURSELF — QUICK GUIDE

Wear cotton underwear.

Change sanitary protection regularly.

After using the lavatory always wipe from front to back.

Get plenty of exercise and fresh air.

Avoid refined foods such as white sugar and white flour, also salt, coffee, tea, alcohol, chocolate, and spices.

Drink plenty of spring water or filtered water during an attack of cystitis, and avoid citrus fruit juices.

Ensure that your diet contains plenty of vitamins A, C, and B-complex, calcium and magnesium.

DEPRESSION

See Chapter 6 for information about winter depression, and the therapeutic use of full spectrum light and supplements. See also Chapter 5 for the benefits of exercise.

DRY SKIN

See the section in this chapter headed Chapped and Cracked Skin.

FEELING CHILLED OR COLD

General feelings of chilliness are often due to poor circulation and can be remedied with exercise; see Chapter 5. Acupressure points may also be stimulated to increase circulation and help the body to create warmth. Point one can be reached and stimulated by yourself, and point two requires a second person.

HOW TO STIMULATE AN ACUPRESSURE POINT

The suggestions in this section involve a harmless stimulation technique of certain acupressure points, using the tip of a thumb, or the soft eraser end of a new eraser-tipped pencil.

Point One

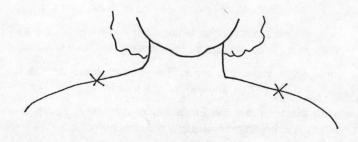

These pressure points are located in the midway point on the top of the shoulders. Use your thumb tip or the eraser at the end of a pencil to stimulate these points. Begin with the right side and probe gently until you feel a twinge of sensitivity in the indicated area. When you locate the correct point, stimulate the area deeply, without rubbing, in a counter-clockwise direction for 15-20 seconds. Apply adequate pressure, but not enough to cause bruising. Next, stimulate the point on the left side in the same way. Relax. The point should not be stimulated more than twice a day.

Point Two

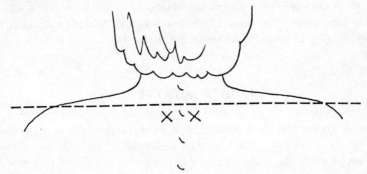

The stimulation of the pressure point should be carried out for you by another person, using the tip of a thumb or the eraser at the end of a pencil. Probe until a twinge of sensitivity is found in the acupressure point on the right. Using adequate pressure, stimulate the point deeply in a counter-clockwise direction for 15-20 seconds. Do not rub. Repeat on the left side. It is not necessary to stimulate these points more than twice a day.

NOTE: It is best to stimulate acupressure points four hours after taking any medicines, herbs, or after drinking alcohol. Allow at least half an hour to elapse after eating a heavy meal, taking strenuous exercise, or having a hot bath. If you are pregnant, or have any heart conditions, cancer or cancerous growths, or scars, warts or moles in the immediate area, avoid using these acupressure points.

RHEUMATIC PAINS

An extremely high percentage of people suffer with some form of rheumatism. It is characterized by soreness in the muscles and joints, and may start as stiffness or pain in certain areas of the body such as the shoulders, thighs, neck, knees, back, or buttocks. Rheumatic pains are often worse in the winter because the cold causes obstruction of the capillaries. This results in decreased circulation, and subsequent accumulation of metabolic waste around joints and muscles. Inactivity, tension, stress, anxiety, and poor posture can all contribute to rheumatic pains by decreasing circulation and metabolism. If you suspect that you may have rheumatism seek help from a doctor or natural practitioner. See Finding a Natural Practitioner in Chapter 11.

SELF-HELP ACTION PLAN

Try to keep your house as warm and dry as possible, and avoid going out when the weather is particularly cold or damp. Never wear damp clothing as this can quickly bring on rheumatic pains. Try to get some exercise every day, as the joints should be moved gently but regularly. For more information on exercise see Chapter 5.

NATURE'S MEDICINE CHEST

External Remedies

☑ Massage painful areas once or twice a day with Rhus tox. ointment, or chamomile oil, comfrey tincture, or thyme oil. To help ease the pain, heat can be applied to the area with a hot water bottle or heating pad.

☑ Dry skin brushing increases general circulation and aids in the body's removal of waste acids via the skin. For instructions on how to skin brush, see Bad Circulation in this chapter.

☑ To reduce pain and swelling a poultice of green clay may be used directly on the sore area overnight. The clay should be mixed in advance, for several days use. Put 4 tablespoons of green clay powder into a non-plastic or metallic bowl. Add enough filtered water to produce a smooth, thin paste. Choose a piece of cotton cloth, a little larger than the area to be treated, and use a wooden spoon to spread an even layer of clay, about ¼ in (6mm) thick, on one side. (Pour a little extra water over the top of the remaining clay in the bowl then cover immediately with cling film.) Apply the bandage, with the clay directly on the skin, making sure that it is pressed down well. Cover the first bandage with a large outer band of warm cloth. Leave on overnight. It may be necessary to use the clay poultice every night for several weeks before significant relief is obtained.

✔ Dead Sea salts can be added to hot water as a soak for rheumatic fingers or hands. The salts are high in minerals and can help to relieve pain. General aches and muscular pains can be helped by adding the salts to a hot bath for a soothing soak.

Treatment From the Inside, Out

Natural practitioners believe that, in many cases, rheumatic pains are caused by accumulation of metabolic residues and acids around the joints and muscles. Good circulation and metabolism play an important role in carrying away these wastes before they have a chance to build up. Exercise is an effective means of encouraging these functions. Since the liver is the clearing-house for poisons, acids, and metabolic wastes, it is possibly the key to prevention, or alleviation of rheumatic pains.

✔ Foods such as dandelion leaves and roots, fresh lemon juice and olive oil used as a salad dressing, artichoke, asparagus, beets, celery, leeks, radishes, onions, garlic, and cabbage support liver function.

✔ Acidophilus powder can be used to help re-establish important bowel flora, improve digestion, and help liver function. Natural 'live' yogurt should be eaten regularly to encourage the growth of acidophilus bacteria.

✔ Wake up your liver and digestive organs before breakfast with a large glass of hot filtered water and fresh lemon juice. Rinse your mouth with plain water immediately after, to preserve your tooth enamel.

✔ Green clay can be used internally as an alternative morning drink but, it should be avoided if you are using homoeopathic or orthodox medicines. At least two weeks before beginning treatment, change to a wholefood diet and avoid coffee, alcohol, and sugar. Drink plenty of fluids such as filtered or mineral water, dandelion root coffee, herbal teas, and grape or black cherry juice.

Prepare the clay before retiring to bed. Stir ½ teaspoon of green clay powder into a glass of filtered water. Remove the spoon immediately, cover and leave overnight. For the first three mornings, do not stir the mixture; drink the liquid but discard the sediment. Eat breakfast 20-30 minutes later. After three days of drinking only the water, the clay may be stirred into the water, and this routine can be continued for three weeks, after which a week should be allowed to elapse. Thereafter alternate a week of treatment with a week of rest. If the clay causes constipation, dissolve it in a larger quantity of water, and do not stir the mixture. You may also find that taking the clay at night prevents this reaction.

✔ The typical diet is too often biased in favour of foods which produce acid when broken down in the body. Sugar and wheat, bread, pies, cereals, cheese, tea, coffee, chocolate, meat, peanuts, and alcohol all fall within this category. If the liver and kidneys are not working as efficiently as they should, acid breakdown products may accumulate around the joints and other tissues. Acids cause irritation and degeneration of connective tissue, which eventually adds up to rheumatic pain.

Change to a wholefood diet and use a variety of grains such as millet, buckwheat, rice, quinoa, and barley rather than wheat. Raw goat milk is high in natural sodium and fluorine; minerals which keep the joints supple. It is an alternative to cow's milk and it also freezes well.

Eat a green salad every day, and generally increase your intake of raw foods, because most have an alkaline reaction in the body. Use the Food Sources Quick Reference Chart in Chapter 3 to increase the variety of foods in your diet, and ensure that you are getting plenty of nutrients, especially vitamins A, B3, B5, B6, C, and E, and the minerals, sodium (not table salt), potassium, zinc, magnesium, and selenium.

✔ Some people find that stopping all nightshade foods for up to six months helps to decrease their arthritic and rheumatic pains. Avoid: aubergine (eggplant), tomatoes, potatoes (except sweet potatoes), and all peppers, and watch for them in pre-made foods. Tobacco also belongs to the nightshade family, and should not be used.

✔ Consumption of citrus fruit juices, except fresh lemon juice, seems to worsen some cases of rheumatism or arthritis. If you regularly drink quantities of grapefruit or orange juice, it may be helpful to limit your intake to whole citrus fruit only, and drink grape or cherry juice instead to help flush accumulated waste acids from your body.

✔ Drinking fresh vegetable juices may be one of the most helpful ways to ease arthritic and rheumatic pains. The high alkalinity of raw vegetable juices helps to dissolve the accumulation of deposits around joints and tissues. If you have a juicer, extract the juice from:

3 large carrots
3 sticks celery
¼ beetroot (small)
½ clove garlic
4 large dandelion leaves
⅛ cucumber (large).

Use organically grown vegetables if you have access to them, and drink the juice once a day, immediately after it has been extracted.

Fresh vegetable juice aids liver function, and is high in minerals, especially potassium and sodium. Organic or plant sodium helps digestion and keeps the joints limber. It also helps to carry inorganic sodium from table salt out of the body, and this is often of great help to arthritis and rheumatism sufferers.

NOTE: the carotenoid pigment in carrots can impart an orange/yellow colouring to the palms of hands, or the soles of feet. This is harmless and will gradually disappear when the source of carotene is reduced or withdrawn.

✔ Homoeopathic tissue salts can be used to help rheumatic pains. Ferr. phos. is used for inflammation, pain, and congestion; Nat. phos. to neutralize acids and aid their elimination; Nat. sulph. to remove toxic fluids from the body; and Silica to break up and eliminate uric acid crystals around muscles and joints.

✔ The homoeopathic remedy Rhus tox. is a general remedy for rheumatism, and Bryonia is used when the pain is aggravated by motion or warmth. Rhododendron is indicated when the pain is worse during weather changes, or when a storm is imminent. Rhus tox. can be taken in tablet form, and used externally as ointment.

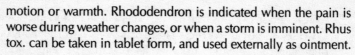 A daily cup of horsetail tea provides plant silica which aids in the elimination of acids, and assists in the proper utilization of calcium.

For some cases of rheumatism, devil's claw tablets, yucca, green lipped mussel, or aloe vera provide relief.

Certain supplements may be helpful, and include: B-complex, vitamins A and D from cod liver oil, vitamin E, zinc, and evening primrose oil. Vitamin C and bioflavonoids may help if taken in small, frequent doses totalling 1000–3000mg a day. Use sodium ascorbate powder for best results.

NOTE: Before using high doses of vitamin C, see Checklist 3 to find out whether any medicine you are taking will interact with it.

HELP YOURSELF — QUICK GUIDE

Stay indoors if the weather is very cold or damp.

Never wear damp clothing, and try to keep warm.

Exercise is very important for good circulation which carries acids away from the joints and muscles.

Eat a wholefood diet.

SORE THROAT

The throat is classified as part of the respiratory system because air passes from the nose or mouth through the throat on its way to the lungs. The throat is at risk from infection, and up to 12 per cent of visits to GPs are in connection with sore throats. This is rarely a serious disorder, but it may indicate an infectious or inflammatory condition elsewhere in the body. A doctor should be consulted if there is severe soreness, bleeding, or if the problem lasts for longer than three days.

Over 95 per cent of sore throats are caused by viruses or bacteria, but anything that irritates the mucous membranes at the back of the throat can cause soreness. In response to an infection, the throat may become inflamed and red, and the glands in the neck may enlarge, because the tonsils and the lymph glands are part of the body's immune system, and this signifies defensive action. For more information about the lymph system see Chapter 2.

SELF-HELP ACTION PLAN

☑ If you are a smoker, try to stop or limit smoking while you have a sore throat. If you cannot stop, try to cut down by smoking fewer cigarettes every day, take fewer puffs at a cigarette, and only smoke it halfway down. Try not to inhale the smoke into your lungs, and choose a low-tar brand. See also Smoking in Chapter 11.

☑ Hot, dry air can irritate the throat and in heated rooms where there is little ventilation it can help to use a humidifier, or leave a bowl of steaming water in the room. Steam can also be used as a soothing inhalation. For instructions see Catarrh in this chapter.

☑ Always try to breathe through your nose, rather than your mouth. The nose has built-in filters which catch micro-organisms and irritants before they reach your throat or lungs.

☑ Wear a silk scarf over your nose, mouth and neck on very cold days. It will act as an air filter, warm the air you breathe in, and keep your whole body warmer by preventing the loss of body heat from the neck area.

NATURE'S MEDICINE CHEST

Treatment From the Inside, Out

☑ Children and adults may safely use homoeopathic remedies, and there are a number of remedies for different types of sore throat.

Aconite is used for laryngitis and sore throat following exposure to cold, dry winds. Apis is used when there are stinging pains in the throat, which appears red and shiny. Belladonna is for a very sore throat with hoarseness and pains which spread to the head. Gelsemium can help colds, flu, and sore throats. If you will be using any of the pungent sore throat remedies in this section, they will neutralize the homoeopathic remedies if used at the same time — allow at least three hours to elapse between them. Homoeopathic tissue salts Calc. phos. and Ferr. phos. are used for laryngitis.

Local and Systemic Remedies

✔ Garlic's antiseptic action kills the micro-organisms responsible for sore throats and throat infection. Peel 1 clove of garlic, crush it, and add to a little warm water and honey. This effective remedy can be used as a gargle or sipped slowly.

✔ Add 1 crushed clove of garlic and ¼ teaspoon cayenne pepper to ¾ pint (425ml) warm filtered water. Mix well, and use as a gargle twice a day.

✔ To help reduce swelling of mucous membranes in the throat suck a small piece of ginger root. If you have a hiatus hernia, avoid ginger as this may cause an uncomfortable burning sensation.

✔ A bitter, pungent tea for sore throats can be made by adding ⅛ teaspoon of cayenne pepper and ½ teaspoon of golden seal powder to hot water. Sip it very slowly. Cayenne increases circulation, and golden seal is helpful for inflammation. Any remedy containing golden seal should be used with caution if you have blood sugar disorders. If you have hypoglycaemia only use this remedy as a gargle.

✔ Zinc gluconate can kill micro-organisms on the membranes of the throat on contact. At the first sign of a sore throat, suck a zinc gluconate tablet, but do not exceed 30mg of zinc per day.

HELP YOURSELF — QUICK GUIDE

If you are a smoker try to stop, or limit smoking.

Use a humidifier in heated rooms to prevent dry air irritating your throat.

A slice of raw garlic kept in the mouth for approximately 15 minutes can help to stop a sore throat.

Always breathe through your nose: it acts as a filter.

At the first sign of a sore throat, suck a zinc gluconate tablet.

Take steps to strengthen your immune system — see Chapters 2 and 3.

CHECKLIST 3   MEDICINES AND VITAMIN C

Before you reach for the vitamin C, use this checklist to find out whether any of the medicines you are currently taking could be affected by supplemental doses of this nutrient.

Medicine	Interaction
Allopurinol anti-gout medicines	Supplemental vitamin C can increase the chance of kidney stones if taken with these medicines.
Anticholineric and antispasmodic medicines	Doses of vitamin C greater than 500mg taken twice a day can decrease the effects of these medicines.
Anticoagulants	Large doses of vitamin C (over 500mg twice a day), taken with anticoagulants, may decrease the effect of the medicine.

Medicine	Interaction
Anxiolytics and tranquillizers	Vitamin C can increase the effects of these medicines and should only be taken in supplement form under medical supervision.
Aspirin and other anti-inflammatory medicines	Vitamin C is depleted by taking these medicines; however, if supplemental vitamin C is used, it should be in the form of calcium ascorbate, to prevent increased stomach irritation.
Oral corticosteriods	Avoid taking vitamin C supplements in doses over 500mg twice a day, unless your doctor advises you to do so.
Paracetamol	No more than 250mg of vitamin C should be taken twice a day when using paracetamol. High doses of vitamin C decrease the excretion of this drug from the body and this could increase the possibility of experiencing side-effects.
The Pill	Avoid taking doses of vitamin C over 250mg twice a day, as a higher intake can increase the availability of oestrogen in the body, which can alter a low-dose Pill to a high-dose, raising the chance of experiencing some oestrogen-related side-effects.
Quinidine anti-arrhythmics	Doses of vitamin C greater than 100-200mg twice a day, can decrease the effects of these medicines.

Medicine	Interaction
Sulphonamides and Trimethoprim	While taking a course of either of these antibiotics, avoid supplemental doses of vitamin C over 250mg a day, as there is a risk of kidney damage.

For further information about drug and nutrient interactions, see *The Medicine Chest* (Thorsons, 1988).

BIBLIOGRAPHY

C. Pinnock et al., 'Vitamin A Status in Children who are Prone to Respiratory Tract Infections', *Australian Paediatric In.* 22, 2, pp.95-9, May 1986.

C. Ashton, 'Caffeine and Health', *British Medical Journal* 21, pp.1293-4, Nov. 1987.

Ananda S. Prasad et al., 'Serum Thymulin and Zinc Deficiency in Humans', *American Journal of Clinical Nutrition* 45, 4, April 1987.

N.W. Solomons, 'The Interaction of Vitamin A and Zinc: Implications for Human Nutrition', *American Journal of Clinical Nutrition* 33, pp.2031-40, 1980.

J.C. Smith Jr et al., 'Alterations in Vitamin A Metabolism During Zinc Deficiency and Food and Growth Restriction', *Journal of Nutrition* 106, pp.569-74, 1976.

B.T. Jones, R.H. Loiselle, 'Reversibility of Serotonin Irritation Syndrome with Atmospheric Anions', *Journal of Clinical Psychiatry* 47, pp.141-3, 1986.

H.M.V. Newton B.Sc., et al., 'The Cause and Correction of Low Blood Vitamin C Concentrations in the Elderly', *American Journal of Clinical Nutrition* 42, 4, pp.656-9, Oct. 1985.

M. Briggs, M. Briggs, 'Vitamin C and Colds', *Lancet* 1, p.998, 1973.

R.G. Smith, M.B., Ch.B., F.R.C.P.E., 'Zinc May be Important in the Elderly Patient's Ability to Resist Infection', *Geriatric Medicine* 17, 7, p.18, 1987.

M.J. Kluger et al., 'Fever and Survival', *Science* 188, pp.166-8, 1975.

M.J. Murray, A.B. Murray, 'Anorexia of Infection as a Mechanism of Host Defence', *American Journal of Clinical Nutrition* 32, pp.593-6, 1979.

M. Taylor Baer, Ph.D., et al., 'Nitrogen Utilization, Enzyme Activity, Glucose Intolerance, and Leukocyte Chemotaxis in Human Experimental Zinc Depletion', *American Journal of Clinical Nutrition* 41, 6, pp.1220-35, 1986.

K.M. Hambridge, 'Zinc and Chromium in Human Nutrition', *Journal of Human Nutrition* 32, pp.99-110, 1978.

F.M. Hess et al., 'Effect of Low Zinc Intake and Oral Contraceptive Agents on Nitrogen Utilization and Clinical Findings in Young Women', *Journal of Nutrition* 107, pp.2219-27, 1977.

R.S. Pekarek et al., 'Abnormal Cellular Immune Responses During Acquired Zinc Deficiency', *American Journal of Clinical Nutrition* 32, pp.1253-9, 1979.

M. Brook, J.J. Grimshaw, 'Vitamin C Concentrations of Plasma and Leukocytes as Related to Smoking Habits, Age, and Sex of Humans', *American Journal of Clinical Nutrition* 21, pp.1254-8, 1968.

C. Pinnock et al., 'Vitamin A Status in Children who are Prone to Respiratory Tract Infections', *Australian Paediatric In.* 22, 2, pp.95-9, May 1986.

J. Bernestine et al., 'Depression of Lymphocyte Transformation Following Oral Glucose Ingestion', *American Journal of Clinical Nutrition* 30, p.613, 1977.

A. Sanchez et al., 'Role of Sugar in Human Neutrophic Phagocytosis', *American Journal of Clinical Nutrition* 26, pp.1180-84, 1973.

W.H. Schuessler, *The Biochemic Handbook*, Thorsons, 1984.

Prof. Hans Fluck, *Medical Plants*, Foulsham.

Carl Pfeiffer Ph.D., M.D., *Mental and Elemental Nutrients*, Keats 1975.

R.C. Wren F.L.S., *Potter's Cyclopaedia of Botanical Drugs and Preparations*, Health Science Press.

Dorothy Hall, *The Book of Herbs*, Pan 1976.

Raymond Dextreit, *Our Earth Our Cure*, Swan House Publishing, 1974.

Gillian Martlew ND and Shelley Silver, *The Medicine Chest*, Thorsons, 1988.

Gillian Martlew ND and Shelley Silver, *The Pill Protection Plan*, Thorsons, 1989.

Chapter 8

TRADITIONAL REMEDIES AND COUNTRY WISDOM

Traditional and folk remedies are often labelled as snake oil and witches' potions, but many of these treatments and tips have been passed down through the generations because they work. It is only since the beginning of this century that they have steadily fallen from favour, probably because of the number of convenient ready-made chemical products on the market. The simple remedies from the hedgerows are disappearing almost as fast as the hedgerows themselves. Some of the remedies and country wisdom in this section are useful alternatives to modern preparations, while others stand alone. Give them a try; you may be surprised to find that remedies used generations ago still work today.

AIR FRESHENER

If a room becomes stuffy, add a few twigs from a rosemary bush to the fire, or burn some in the grate. Rosemary acts as an instant air freshener.

CARING FOR WOOLLENS

Vinegar and Glycerine Fabric Softener
Winter woollens will feel softer if you add a teaspoonful of vinegar to the next but last rinse, and half a teaspoon of glycerine to the last rinse.

CHAPPED SKIN

Honey Moisturizer
Honey has antiseptic, healing, and moisturizing qualities and can help to soothe chapped skin. Wash your face or hands with warm water, towel dry gently, and apply a layer of honey to the skin. Leave on for about 15 minutes then rinse with warm water.

Honey, Egg and Barley Mask
Your skin will appreciate this wholesome face mask which softens and soothes winter-worn skin. Mix together the white of one egg, 1 oz (28g) of honey, and 3 oz (84g) of barley flour, until a paste is formed. Apply it to your face, avoiding the eyes and neck, and rinse off with warm water after about 15–20 minutes.

Soap Alternative
Washing chapped hands with soap dries the skin and makes the condition more painful. The alternative is to wash your hands with oatmeal and water. Dry your hands carefully after washing, and then rub them with a little dry oatmeal.

Home-Made Handcream
Mix together equal parts of honey, rose water, glycerine, and lemon juice to create an old fashioned hand lotion. (Glycerine and rose water are obtainable from some chemists or health stores). Put the lotion into a bottle, and leave it in the kitchen or bathroom. For best results use it while the hands are still damp.

CHILBLAINS

Onion Balm
Try rubbing chilblains with a piece of freshly cut onion; it will help to stop them itching.

Bran Mash

More than three centuries ago this remedy was used to help soothe chilblains. It can be made simply by mixing a tablespoon of wheat bran with enough water to form a paste. Allow the mixture to soak for about five minutes, and then apply it to the chilblain. If it is at the throbbing and itching stage, the bran and water paste will soothe it, and if broken, it will help to heal it.

Shoe Tips

Tight footwear or socks decrease circulation, and this is the main reason for the appearance of chilblains when the temperature drops. If you wear more than one pair of socks on very cold days make sure that your shoes or boots can accommodate the extra layers comfortably.

CIRCULATION

Ginger Punch

Add some piquancy to your winter cooking by grating some fresh ginger root into your stews, casseroles, and soups. Ginger helps to increase circulation and imparts a warm afterglow.

COLD FEET

Cayenne Cure

If you suffer from cold feet in the winter, here is a trick to put fire in your boots. Sprinkle some cayenne pepper into your shoes or wellies and your feet will not turn blue. However, they will turn red/orange as the cayenne contains a coloured pigment, which will dye your socks and the inside of your footwear — so wear old shoes and socks when using cayenne.

Mustard Soak

Coming in from the cold with icy feet can result in agony as the feet begin to re-warm. Speed up the process by dissolving a dessertspoon of ordinary mustard powder in 4 pints (2¼ litres) of warm, but not hot, water. Soak your feet in the tingly warmth for up to 15 minutes, adding a little hot water at intervals to maintain the temperature. Towel dry and put on a thick pair of dry, warm socks, and slippers.

NOTE: Do not use either of these remedies if you suffer from sensitive skin, or if you have any cuts or sores on your feet, they may cause an uncomfortable burning sensation.

COLDS AND FLU

Onion and Catnip Broth
As soon as you feel a cold coming on have some hot home-made onion and catnip broth. This is prepared by dicing 4 large onions and adding them to 2 pints (1 litre) of water in a non-aluminium saucepan. Add *Vecon* or vegetable seasoning to taste, and bring to the boil. Reduce to a simmer and cook for 15 minutes. While this is cooking, take 2 tablespoons of catnip herb, and pour 1 pint of boiling water over it. Allow to steep for five minutes, then strain and add to the broth. One or two steaming bowls of onion and catnip broth should stop a cold in its tracks.

Chicken Soup
Drinking warm liquids helps to relieve congestion, and chicken soup contains a substance which further increases this action. In order to function properly the immune system needs a constant supply of nutrients and protein, and chicken soup is rich in protein. However, avoid croûtons and other accompaniments made from wheat as these can encourage mucus during a cold. For increased expectorant effects add plenty of garlic and onions to the recipe.

Propolis Remedy
Propolis is a substance which bees gather from the buds and bark of certain trees, and use as a 'glue' for their hives. It is a mixture of many compounds including nutrients and an anti-bacterial substance. Propolis is mentioned in medicine as far back as the first century AD. It has been

used particularly as a remedy for slow healing sores and ulcers, and as a potent anti-bacterial, anti-viral and anti-fungal agent which also enhances the immune system. Propolis can be used safely by young and old to help prevent a cold, or to remedy a sore throat. Contact a local bee keeper and ask if you can buy some propolis. Take a small nugget and hold it in the mouth until it dissolves. This can be repeated as many times as necessary throughout the day.

Garlic
Garlic contains a sulphur compound called allicin which prevents the growth of micro-organisms in the body. It also contains the immune-boosting minerals selenium and germanium. It is one of the strongest and best anti-infective agents known to us and has been used medicinally for centuries. Garlic is best eaten fresh, although crushed, cooked garlic is quite effective. Use up to three cloves a day to prevent or remedy infections and sore throats.

COLD WRISTS

Why is it that gloves and sleeves never quite meet in the middle, and there is always a draught round the wrists? The cure for this is to find an old pair of long socks, cut off the feet, and make a thumb hole in each, about 3 inches (8cm) from the bottom. Slip the wrist warmers on and then add coat and gloves. These are especially good for keeping children's hands and wrists warm when they play in the snow.

CONGESTION AND COUGH

At the time of the year when coughs and congestion are most common, nature provides the remedy. Pick some fresh, ripe rose hips, wash them well and put them in a non-aluminium saucepan with enough water to just cover them. Bring to the boil, add some honey, and simmer for at least 20 minutes. Strain, and sip a cupful of the liquid as needed.

If the cough or congestion becomes severe, or if there is no improvement within three days, always consult your doctor.

Baked Lemon Cough Remedy
For coughs or colds, people used to take the juice from a baked lemon. Why this helps is a mystery, but when properly prepared it seems to be quite an effective remedy. Bake the lemon in the oven at a moderate heat until it begins to crack open and the juice starts to exude; this may take 1–2 hours. Take 1 teaspoon of the juice, sweetened with a little honey, before each meal, and before retiring to bed. If necessary, it may be taken every 3–4 hours.

Linseed Cough Remedy
To help remedy coughs and colds make an infusion by adding one teaspoon of crushed linseeds to a pint of boiling water. Allow to steep for ten minutes and then slowly sip a cupful every three hours.

Traditional Cough Syrup
Add 1 oz (28g) of grated horseradish root, and 3 oz (85g) of horehound herb to a pint of water. Bring to a boil, then reduce to a simmer and cook until the mixture is reduced by half. Strain and add approximately 4 oz (113g) of honey to the fluid. The resulting cough syrup can be taken in doses of 1 teaspoonful up to four times a day. Avoid this if you have a hiatus hernia as it may cause uncomfortable burning.

EARACHE

Earaches should be reported to your doctor without delay, but until you can actually get to the doctor there are some traditional remedies which may help. If the earache seems to be caused by an infection, it can be helped by placing half a large clove of garlic into a piece of clean gauze, and placing it in the ear, but do not put it in the actual ear canal. Garlic's antiseptic action can help to combat the infection. For a general earache place a warm object against the ear, or alternatively fill a small, clean cotton bag with salt and hold it against the pain.

EMERGENCY INSULATION ON A COLD DAY

Newspaper, although inky, is a very efficient insulator, so if you are caught in the great outdoors with inadequate clothing, use a newspaper as insulation between you and the wind or cold.

FIRE LIGHTERS

Save and dry your orange, grapefruit, and lemon peel because it contains an inflammable oil which can be used to help make lighting the fire easier. Add a few pieces of dried peel to the layers as you make up the fire and they will help to encourage the wood to catch alight.

REMEDIAL COUNTRY WINES

Rural village life of less than a century ago could be very hard, but country folk had their medicinal wines to see them cheerfully through winter's illnesses and ailments. No pantry was complete without special wines prized for their medicinal qualities. If you make your own wine, try adding a medicinal stock to your cellar. The following wines should be taken warmed in 2–4 oz (55–110ml) doses once or twice a day as needed.

- Mulled elderflower wine for sweating out a cold.
- Clover wine for congested breathing.
- Agrimony wine to help rheumatism.

SORE THROAT

Vinegar Gargle
Cider vinegar is an age-old preventative and treatment for colds and sore throats. It can be used as a gargle when a teaspoonful is added to a cup of water. Gargle with a mouthful of the solution, swallow it, then repeat. This can be repeated every hour, until relief is obtained.

If the sore throat is severe or if there is any bleeding, consult your doctor immediately.

Marsh Mallow Throat Balm

Place 1 oz (28g) of marsh mallow root in a cup and pour boiling water over it, allow to steep for five minutes, then add a little honey. The soothing mixture can be used as a gargle several times a day.

Salt Water Gargle

A salt and water gargle will also be effective because salt has anti-bacterial qualities. Add about half a teaspoon of salt to a glass of warm water, and use as a gargle whenever necessary. However, avoid swallowing the mixture as it could make you feel sick.

Propolis

For information about propolis see the propolis remedy under Colds and Flu in this chapter.

BIBLIOGRAPHY

Fairfax Family, *Arcana Fairfariana Manuscripta*, Mawson, Swan and Morgan, 1890.

Godfrey Baseley, *A Country Compendium*, Sidgwick and Jackson, 1977.

D.C. Jarvis MD, *Folk Medicine*, Pan, 1971.

Chapter 9

MEDICINES AND WINTER

MEDICINES AND BODY TEMPERATURE

Almost everyone who takes medicines has, at some time, experienced side-effects. Occasionally adverse drug reactions can be mistaken for other problems, or they may not appear to be linked to a drug at all. This is particularly true with a number of drugs that can affect our ability to tolerate the cold; some may increase sensitivity to extreme temperature changes, while others may cause an actual drop in body temperature. One group of drugs commonly causes cold hands and feet by constriction of peripheral blood vessels.

The elderly tend to be more vulnerable to the adverse effects of medicines because, as the body ages, drugs are used and eliminated more slowly. The longer a drug stays in the body the more chance there is of experiencing side-effects or interactions between different medicines.

It has been said that it takes an hour longer to break down a drug for every year that we have lived, so a healthy person aged 20 will usually metabolize and eliminate a dose of medicine in about 20 hours, while someone in their 70s may need up to three days to complete the same process.

The factors which lead to this cause a gradual build-up of the drug in the system and there are three major reasons why this happens. First, the liver's metabolism of medicines decreases with age, and secondly, time also takes its toll on the kidneys which are the main route of drug elimination. Both the liver and kidneys may be coping sufficiently with natural body wastes, but the extra load created by taking drugs may prove to be too much so that the residues are not eliminated as thoroughly as they should be sure. Thirdly, the level of a special protein in the blood called albumin decreases in concentration as we age. Albumin tends to have an important limiting effect on drugs because it binds with them but lower blood levels of this protein leaves drugs virtually unbound and this may lead to adverse reactions to medicines, even those that have been taken previously with no apparent side-effects.

By using Checklist 4, Drugs and Body Temperature, you can find out whether one of the drugs you are taking could have side-effects which may leave you feeling colder. If you suspect that your drug is causing this reaction, and it is making you feel uncomfortable, ask your pharmacist or doctor for advice. DO NOT stop taking the drug unless directed to do so by your doctor. This is vitally important because many of the drugs which can have these side-effects are used for the heart, and discontinuing them may seriously endanger your health.

CHECKLIST 4 DRUGS AND BODY TEMPERATURE

Drug Group	Possible Side-Effects	Common/ Infreq/Rare	Special Information
BETA BLOCKERS Used mainly for heart and circulation disorders	Cold hands and feet Sensitivity to cold	▲ ▲ ▲	These side-effects may be increased if other anti-hypertensive drugs are taken with beta blockers
NITRATE VASODILATORS	Cold skin	▲	These side-effects may be increased if other vasodilators are taken with nitrate vasodilators
VASODILATORS Used for circulation disorders, cramps and ulcers	There may be an increased sensitivity to temperature changes	▲	These side-effects may be increased if other vasodilators or beta blockers are taken with vasodilators. If you will be taking a winter holiday to a very warm climate, tell your doctor, as you may be

Drug Group	Possible Side-Effects	Common/ Infreq/Rare	Special Information
			very sensitive to the temperature change
ANTICONVULSANTS Used mainly for epilepsy and seizures	Prolonged or continued treatment may cause a drop in body temperature	▲	These side-effects may be increased if antidiabetic drugs are taken with anticonvulsants
ANTINAUSEANTS This applies to prochlorperazine only	Possible risk of sensitivity to extreme temperature changes	▲	If you will be taking a winter holiday to a very warm climate, tell your doctor, as you may be very sensitive to the temperature change
MIGRAINE AND HEADACHE MEDICINES	Cold skin	▲	The over 60s may be particularly susceptible to circulation disorders such as coldness, tingling, numbness, or 'pins and needles' of the extremities
ASPIRIN	Anaemia	▲	Because of the possibility of stomach irritation and bleeding with the frequent and regular use of aspirin, there may be the rare possibility of anaemia developing, especially in the elderly, or people whose diet is unsatisfactory. Anaemia can leave you feeling colder. If alcohol is taken with aspirin it can increase the stomach irritation and bleeding. As a precaution, up to

Drug Group	Possible Side-Effects	Common/ Infreq/Rare	Special Information
			500mg per day of vitamin C can be taken in the form of *calcium ascorbate*, and this will help to decrease the risk of stomach bleeding
Key: Common ▲▲		Infrequent or rare ▲	

MEDICINES AND IMMUNE NUTRIENTS

If the immune system is strong, winter does not have to be a battlefield of seasonal ills and ailments. However, with the fluctuations in weather and spending more time indoors, we can become more vulnerable to illness. Taking long-term courses of certain medicines may increase vulnerability to infection. This is because a number of them interfere with the way the body uses vitamins and minerals, some of which are vital to immune system health. The elderly, some vegans, women using the contraceptive pill, and dieters may be most affected. Illness in the elderly is very often accompanied by loss of appetite, so it is very important to check that nutritional requirements are met, particularly if medicines are being taken.

Drugs relieve symptoms of illness, but they may actually interfere with the body's immune system. For instance, certain medicines used for colds stop the flow of mucus which is vital for the excretion of infecting organisms. This can lead to their retention and further infection.

A number of drugs can lower the immune response directly, by decreasing the amount of infection-fighting white blood cells in the body. These include: corticosteroids, erythromycin, indomethacin, and tricyclic antidepressants.

The following chart will help you to find out whether your medicine could be depleting some of the most important immune system nutrients. Losses tend to occur mainly with long term use, or with very high dosages, so if you are taking a short course of tablets this is unlikely to be significant. To ensure that your diet contains plenty of foods which can compensate nutrient depletion, check the Food Sources Quick Reference Chart in Chapter 3.

MEDICINES WHICH MAY DECREASE THE MAIN IMMUNE NUTRIENTS

Type of medicine	Nutrient affected
ANTACIDS	Vitamin A Vitamin B1 vitamin B2 vitamin B6 vitamin B12 folic acid vitamin C
ANTICONVULSANTS	vitamin B12 calcium magnesium vitamin C
ANTIDEPRESSANTS	vitamin B2
ANTIHISTAMINES	vitamin C
ANTI-INFLAMMATORIES (NON-STEROIDAL)	iron vitamin C vitamin B1
ANTIPARKINSONIAN MEDICINES	vitamin B3 vitamin B6* vitamin B12 folic acid

Type of medicine	Nutrient affected
ANTITHYROID MEDICINES	calcium magnesium
ASPIRIN AND ASPIRIN-BASED MEDICINES	vitamin A vitamin B1 vitamin B12 vitamin C calcium magnesium
CONTRACEPTIVES (ORAL)	vitamin B2 vitamin B6 vitamin B12 vitamin C folic acid zinc magnesium
CORTISONE	vitamin B6 folic acid vitamin C zinc calcium
DIGITALIS MEDICINES	zinc magnesium
DIURETICS	B-complex vitamins vitamin C zinc calcium magnesium

(continued overleaf) ▶

Type of medicine	Nutrient affected
LIPID LOWERING MEDICINES	vitamin A vitamin B12 folic acid vitamin E
PENICILLINS AND RELATED MEDICINES	vitamin A vitamin B1 vitamin B6 vitamin B12 biotin vitamin C
SULPHONAMIDES	vitamin B1 vitamin B3 vitamin B6 vitamin B12 vitamin C* biotin folic acid** PABA** calcium magnesium
TETRACYCLINES	vitamin A vitamin B1 vitamin B2 vitamin B6 vitamin B12 folic acid vitamin C zinc calcium magnesium

Type of medicine	Nutrient affected
URINARY TRACT ANTI-INFECTIVES	vitamin B1 folic acid biotin

* Avoid daily doses of more than 250mg of vitamin C. Larger doses may result in damage to the kidneys when taking sulphonamides.
** Avoid taking supplements of these nutrients with these medicines. The supplements will decrease the medicines's effectiveness.
(See also Checklist 5 for details of drugs which may affect your balance.)

DRUGS, WINTER AND VITAMIN D

During the winter we are exposed to less sunlight, and as a result the body does not manufacture very much of its own vitamin D. If dietary choices lead to a low intake of this nutrient from food, then there is the possibility of suffering from a deficiency through the darkest months of the winter. Those who are most at risk include some vegans, vegetarians, the elderly, and people using the following medicines on a regular basis:

antacids
anticonvulsants
anxiolytics
barbiturates
hypnotics
lipid lowering drugs

For more information about how to counteract vitamin D deficiency if you do not eat animal foods, see Chapter 3.

If you are taking any medicines and are concerned about using large doses of vitamin C with them, see Checklist 3 in Chapter 7 for more information.

BIBLIOGRAPHY

Daphne A. Roe and T. Colin Campbell (Eds), *Drugs and Nutrients*, Vol. 21: The Interactive Effects, Drugs and the Pharmaceutical Sciences, Marcel Dekker Inc., 1984.

Daphne A. Roe (Ed.), *Drugs and Nutrition in the Elderly Patient,* Churchill Livingstone, 1984.

Daphne A. Roe (Ed.), *Drug Induced Nutritional Deficiences* (2nd Edn).

Drug, Nutrient Interrelationships, Nutrition and Pharmacology, an Interphase of Disciplines, Nutrition Society of Canada, McMaster University, Hamilton, 1974.

Gillian Martlew and Shelley Silver, *The Medicine Chest,* Thorsons, 1988.

Gillian Martlew and Shelley Silver, *The Pill Protection Plan,* Thorsons, 1989.

Chapter 10

OVER 60, HOUSE-BOUND, OR DISABLED?

In the winter many of the difficulties, and suffering, encountered by retired people are primarily due to lack of finances, and inadequate housing. Sufficient heating and nutrition can take such a large slice from the budget that, out of necessity, they may be compromised. This increases the danger of suffering from the effects of cold and malnutrition, but, given the right resources, many difficulties that are related to winter can be overcome.

WHERE TO TURN FOR HELP

The following groups and services provide help for people who are finding it difficult to cope with the many problems of winter.

In the USA you can ring Social Security or the Department of Welfare and ask what help is available.

AGE CONCERN

Age Concern
Information and Policy Department
Bernard Sunley House
60 Pitcairn Road
Mitcham
Surrey CR4 3LL
Telephone (01) 640 5431

Age Concern is a registered charity which was founded in 1940 to provide advice and information for the elderly on many different issues, including those specifically linked with winter. There are 29 factsheets available from the Information and Policy Department and they cover a wide range of subjects including heating, housing and accommodation, companions and living-in help, benefits, and telephone costs. The full set of 29 factsheets cost £3.00.

A single copy of Factsheet 1 — Help with Heating, and a copy of Warmth in Winter, can be obtained by sending your request along with a (9" ×6") stamped addressed envelope to the Information and Policy Department. Age Concern also publish books on money, health, housing, diet, and many other subjects.

If you would like more information about the help, advice, and reading material available to you, contact your local Age Concern group listed in the telephone book under 'Age Concern' or 'Old People's Welfare Council'. If you are unable to find a listing, ask at your local library or Citizens Advice Bureau, or write to Age Concern's Information and Policy Department.

For details about Age Concern's electricity and/or gas meter insurance scheme (available in the UK), contact your local Age Concern Group, or write to Alexander Stenhouse (UK) Ltd, Grosvenor House, 45–71 London Road, Redhill, Surrey RH1 1YN.

DISABLED LIVING FOUNDATION

Disabled Living Foundation
380–384 Harrow Road
London W9 2HU
Telephone (01) 289 6111

The Disabled Living Foundation is a registered charity that works to decrease the handicapping effects of disability by finding non-medical solutions to the daily living problems facing disabled people of all ages. Its main activities are research and information provision.

Information and advisory services provide data on equipment, technical aids, services, benefits, design criteria, and legislation. The D.L.F. also provides a comprehensive range of inexpensive resource papers. For more information and details of membership, telephone, or write enclosing an S.A.E.

HELP THE AGED

Information Desk
Help the Aged
St James's Walk
London EC1R OBE
Telephone (01) 253 0253

Help the Aged is a national charity dedicated to improving the quality of life of elderly people in need of help in the UK and overseas. It pursues this aim by raising and granting funds towards community based projects, housing, and overseas aid.

NEIGHBOURHOOD ENERGY ACTION

National Office:
Neighbourhood Energy Action
2nd Floor
2/4 Bigg Market
Newcastle upon Tyne
NE1 1UW
Telephone (091) 261 5677

To get in touch with the energy project in your area, write to:
Monergy Saver
Freepost
Newcastle upon Tyne
NE1 1BR
Telephone: freephone (0800) 234 800

Neighbourhood Energy Action (N.E.A.) is a national charity which supports a network of over 450 local energy projects. N.E.A. projects provide draught-proofing, insulation, and energy advice services to lower income households. N.E.A. receives financial support from the Department of Energy and the Department of the Environment.

WINTER WARMTH LINE

If you have any questions about heating, or keeping your house warm this winter, there is a free hotline you can call in Britain. The Winter Warmth Line, (0800) 289 404, is a free hotline which operates from mid-November to the end of March. It was set up in co-operation with the Government and is backed by a grant from the Department of Health and Social Security. It is run primarily by Help The Aged who are responsible for the day-to-day running, but it is jointly organized with Age Concern and Neighbourhood Energy Action.

SERVICES AND ADVICE FROM THE FUEL INDUSTRY

For details of services that the fuel industries can provide, contact your local gas or electricity showroom. The address is in the telephone book under 'electricity' or 'gas'.

If you have received a fuel bill that seems unreasonable or incorrect, contact the Gas or Electricity Consumer's Council immediately and ask to speak to someone about it. The address will appear on the back of the bill. If the bill is correct, but you will have difficulty paying it, then it may be possible for your local office to arrange payments.

As a pensioner you may be entitled to help. Contact your local DHSS office (in the telephone book under 'Health and Social Security'), or Social Services in the USA, and enquire about the social fund, income support, and fuel direct. If you are threatened with cut-off, contact the fuel board immediately and explain your situation.

British Gas produce a publication called *Getting the Best from Gas: Advice for Senior Citizens*. This booklet contains information ranging from use of employee identity cards, to what to do if there is a gas leak. Copies are available, free of charge, from:

Public Relations Department
British Gas PLC
Rivermill House
152 Grosvenor Road
London SW1V 3JL.

SPECIAL INFORMATION

KEEPING YOUR BALANCE — AVOIDING FALLS

The sense of balance may decline with age, and this can increase the possibility of falling. A number of prescription medicines can quite commonly cause such side-effects as dizziness or lightheadedness, and because drug residues tend to stay in the body longer as we become older, there may be more chance of experiencing side-effects. Checklist 5 can be used to see if any of the medicines you are currently taking could be affecting your balance, or making you feel dizzy or lightheaded.

CHECKLIST 5   MEDICINES AND BALANCE

The side-effects listed in this checklist may only occur during the first few days of treatment with a specific medicine, but if you continue to experience any of them, contact your pharmacist or doctor and ask for advice.

Type of Medicine	Common Side-Effect
Alcohol based over-the-counter medicines	Dizziness. These medicines may interact with anticoagulants, and tranquillizers by increasing all their effects
Anti-arrhythmics	Dizziness
Anticonvulsants	Dizziness
Antidepressants	Dizziness
Antihistamines	Dizziness
Antihypertensives	Dizziness
Antivirals	Lightheadedness/faintness
Anxiolytics	Dizziness/lightheadedness

Type of Medicine	Common Side-Effect
Barbiturates	These drugs may cause night-time falls. If you get up in the night the drugs will have loosened muscles and slowed breathing, so you may be sluggish and dizzy
Beta blockers	Dizziness, although this is infrequent with Labetalol
Diuretics	May directly affect balance in the elderly, so treatment is usually restricted to 2–4 weeks for the elderly or frail
Paracetamol/Acetaminophen	Dizziness
Parasite and worm medicines	Dizziness
Sleeping pills	Dizziness/lightheadedness

If you do find that you feel dizzy, or lose your balance easily, there are some simple precautions that can help to prevent accidents or falls.

✔ If you have periods of dizziness or unsteadiness, use a walking stick around the house to provide support.

✔ Check that all carpets and rugs are secure, and there are no loose corners to trip you.

✔ Try to avoid storing items in cupboards which have to be reached with steps or a stool, as heights can sometimes precipitate dizziness or giddiness and this may lead to a fall.

✔ If possible keep a spare pair of glasses accessible in case your main pair is broken or lost. Difficulty in seeing when moving around the house could result in a fall or accident.

✔ During very windy weather it is wise to avoid shopping with a bag on wheels. These are very light when unladen and if caught by a high wind they can very easily trip you or pull you over.

✔ If you are a smoker, this may be contributing to feelings of dizziness. It is possible that taking a herbal yeast tonic, such as *Bio Strath*, may help dizziness in some cases.

SPECIAL FOOD TIPS

✔ There may be days when it is not possible to go out shopping, particularly if you are elderly or ill, because icy pavements, deep snow, wind, rain, or extreme cold make the journey too hazardous. It is at times like this that a store cupboard containing nutritious food plays an important part in your ability to stay warm and healthy. Extreme winter weather, the kind which stops you going out, puts your health under the greatest strain, and this is just when you need the most nutritious food. See Chapter 3 for more details.

✔ An irregular, scant and low-nutrition diet can leave you feeling colder in the winter. See Chapter 3 for more information.

✔ Sometimes the ability to absorb nutrients from the food we eat decreases as we go through life, and appetite may also decrease. Because of this it is always important to choose enjoyable, nutritious foods. Sometimes it may be necessary to take some supplements, and for more information see Chapters 3 and 9.

✔ In the winter we are exposed to a lower level of sunlight, especially if housebound, and unless the diet is well supplied with foods high in vitamin D, there is the danger of a deficiency developing. Prolonged lack of this nutrient, in conjunction with too little calcium and magnesium, can result in brittle bones. For more information see Chapter 3.

✔ Illness is often accompanied by a loss of appetite and if this happens to you try to eat some vegetable soup for one or two days, until the appetite returns. Sprinkling wheatgerm over the soup just before you eat it adds concentrated nutrients. The herbal food supplement *Bio Strath* aids immune function in addition to stimulating the appetite, as does the mineral zinc. If the loss of appetite continues for more than three days, contact your doctor.

EXERCISE, SUNLIGHT, AND FRESH AIR

Exercise is just as important to health as good food. Lack of exercise can lead to feelings of depression, exhaustion, coldness, aches, and weakness. A pleasant walk in the fresh air increases oxygen intake and stimulates the circulation and appetite. Sunlight can lift the spirits, and if you are feeling depressed a walk may often help.

BIBLIOGRAPHY

Age Concern *Fact Sheet Number 1: Help With Heating*, April 1988.

Warmth in Winter, Age Concern, (amended June 1988).

A.D. Simons, et al., 'Exercise as a Treatment of Depression: an Update', Psychological Reviews 5, pp. 553–68, 1985.

E.W. Martinsen, et al., 'Effects of Aerobic Exercise on Depression', British Medical Journal 291, p. 109, 1985.

Gillian Martlew and Shelley Silver, *The Medicine Chest*, Thorsons, 1988.

Chapter 11

ASSOCIATIONS AND SPECIALIZED PRODUCTS

The following information is intended only as a guide. The first section lists the names and addresses of organizations and associations which provide specific help and information on different areas of health. The second section lists companies that manufacture, or distribute, ecological or specialized products for around the home.

INFORMATION AND SERVICES

FINDING A NATURAL PRACTITIONER

Institute for Complementary Medicine
21 Portland Place
London W1N 3AF

This is a registered charity which can provide information on practitioners and complementary medicine, either on a national or local level. They can also provide details of special courses for medical students, nurses, and other groups. There is a team of highly trained complementary practitioners and a medical doctor. Please send a stamped, self-addressed envelope with any enquiries.

In the USA you might try one of the following associations:

American Association of Naturopathic Physicians
P.O. Box 33046
Portland, OR 97233
Telephone (503) 225-4863

American Holistic Medical Association
2727 Fairview Avenue East
No. G
Seattle, WA 98102
Telephone (206) 322-6842

ENERGY — HELP AND INFORMATION

Neighbourhood Energy Action
Monergy Saver
Freepost
Newcastle upon Tyne NE1 1BR

Neighbourhood Energy Action (N.E.A.) is a British charity that promotes and supports the development nationally of community-based projects which provide draught-proofing, insulation, and energy advice services to lower income households.

For a free 'Monergy Pack', which contains detailed information about heating and insulation, telephone (01) 691 9000, or write to The Department of Energy, Energy Efficiency Office, Blackhorse Road, London SE99 6TT.

MEALS ON WHEELS

Run by the Women's Royal Voluntary Services, this service can bring hot meals to your home. The address of your local group will appear in the telephone directory. A similar provision may be found in the USA by contacting local welfare services.

To qualify for meals on wheels, you have to be recommended by your doctor, or Social Services. Check with them to see whether you are entitled to it.

SAD ASSOCIATION

Mrs Jennifer Eastwood
51 Bracewell Road
London W10 6AF
Telephone (01) 969 7028

The SAD Association is a self-help organization for SAD sufferers and their relatives. Its aims are to promote awareness of SAD and alleviation of the suffering it causes. SADA sends information to enquirers, produces a regular newsletter, makes local contacts and forms discussion groups throughout the country, and offers support and advice to people who need it. SADA also publicizes the illness through the national and local press and media and sends information to health professionals and organizations. Telephone, or write, enclosing a stamped addressed envelope for information and membership details. Members receive a quarterly newsletter and the latest medical and consumer information, plus a list of contacts.

The US address is:

NOSAD

National Organisation for Seasonal Affective Disorder

PO Box 40133, Washington DC 20016

See also Full Spectrum Lighting on page 200.

SMOKING

Action on Smoking and Health
5–11 Mortimer Street
London W1N 7RH
Telephone (01) 637 9843

This is a charitable organization which gathers information on the dangers of smoking, and offers advice on how to stop. It was set up by the Royal College of Physicians, London. For further details, send a stamped, self-addressed envelope with your enquiry. A 'Give-Up' pack is available free of charge. Send a 20 pence-stamped addressed envelope (9″×6″) to the above address.

TELEPHONE INFORMATION — MEDICAL AND HEALTH PROBLEMS

Healthline
18 Victoria Park Square
London E2 9PF
Telephone (01) 980 4848

This organization provides a telephone service that gives detailed information on a wide range of medical and health problems. There are over 200 different recordings which also include information on self-help groups relating to your problem. Some of these tapes offer information on symptoms, treatment, and how to seek proper medical advice. There is no charge for the information and all calls are charged as an ordinary telephone call. Write to Healthline for a booklet containing details of the subjects and numbers to call; please send a stamped, self-addressed envelope with any enquiries.

ECOLOGICAL AND SPECIALIZED HOUSEHOLD PRODUCTS

BIODEGRADABLE HOUSEHOLD CLEANERS

Ecover
Full Moon
Steyning
Sussex BN4 3DG
Telephone (0903) 815 614

Ecover products are an effective range of all-natural household cleansers. They are not tested on animals, contain no phosphates, enzymes, alkalis, optical whiteners, soda ash, or chemical bleaches, and will fully biodegrade within five days. Ecover products are available in most health food shops and in some large supermarket chains.

The product range includes washing-up liquid, wool wash, washing powder, cream cleaner, toilet cleaner, fabric conditioner, floor soap, and heavy duty hand cleaner.

The US address is:
4 Old Mill Road
PO Box 1140
Georgetown
CT 06829-1140

Faith Products
22 Great King Street
Edinburgh EH3 6QH
Telephone (031) 661 0900

Faith Products, Clearspring washing-up liquid and Clearspring laundry liquid, are fully biodegradable and vegan; they are not tested on animals, and are free of alkalis, phosphates, bleaches, optical whiteners, soda ash, and enzymes.

DEAD SEA MINERAL SALTS

Finders Dead Sea Health Company
Winchet Hill
Goudhurst
Cranbrook
Kent TN17 1JY
Telephone (0580) 211055

If you have any difficulty finding Dead Sea mineral salts in your local health store, contact Finders for information about your nearest stockist, or how to order direct.

USA:
West Coast Mineral Corp
7338 Varna Avenue Number 6
North Hollywood
CA 91605

EXERCISE EQUIPMENT

Rebounders
PT Leisure
57 Courthouse Road
Maidenhead
Berks.
Telephone (0628) 28841

Top quality rebounders in the medium price range can be obtained from PT Leisure. Rebounders are available in two sizes, and in a variety of colours. There is also a stabilizer bar available for the larger rebounder. PT Leisure also supply other types of exercise equipment.

FULL SPECTRUM LIGHT TUBES

Full Spectrum Lighting
Unit 4
Wye Trading Estate
London Road
High Wycombe
Bucks HP11 1LH
Telephone (0494) 448727

This company supplies full spectrum light tubes which can be used in standard fluorescent tube fittings. They are available in sizes ranging from 18 inches to 8 feet (45–240cm). FSL welcomes enquiries, by phone or letter, and will also provide advice and information on SAD. They also manufacture the special light boxes used in the medical research on SAD.

In the USA, full spectrum light tubes may be obtained from:
Vitalite
Commercial Engineering
Duro-Test Corporation
2321 Kennedy Boulevard
North Bergen
New Jersey 07047

GREEN CLAY

Mayflower Beauty Products
Island Farm Avenue
Molesey Trading Estate
Surrey KT8 OUZ
Telephone (01) 979 7261

If you are unable to obtain green clay at your local health store, contact

Mayflower Beauty Products for details of your nearest stockist.

USA
Pierre Cattier Clay Products
Three Sheaves Co Inc
Distributers
New York, NY 10013

IONIZER AND AIR PROCESSOR MANUFACTURERS

All 13 amp plugs used with ionizers should be fitted with a 3 amp fuse.

Amcor
Amcor House
19 Woodfield Road
London W9 2BA
Telephone (01) 289 4433

Amcor USA
5–39, 46th Avenue
Long Island City
NY 11101
Telephone (718) 361-2700

Amcor has a wide range of ionizers including two domestic models, the pyramid shaped *Freshen Aire* and the *Air Processor* which filters and ionizes the air. Amcor also manufacture commercial and home air processors, elecrostatic air cleaners, and dehumidifiers. The dust trap is also available for use with some models of ionizers and will catch the dust, soot and other pollutants that are drawn from the air. The Freshen Aire produces negative irons by using carbon fibres, not probes or needles as with other ionizers. The units include a high and low on/off switch. Amcor will answer telephone or written queries.

ClearAir UK
P.O. Box 83
Covent Garden
London WC2H 9AJ
Telephone (01) 379 7369

ClearAir produce the VM ionizer which is efficient and reasonably priced. It conforms to British Safety Standard BS 3456. The ionizer is supplied with a plug and 3 amp fuse. ClearAir donate 20p of each sale to research into the prevention of asthma in children. ClearAir will supply a comprehensive consumer package on request.

LEDA

Leek Electrical Domestic Applicances
Dairy House
Ford
Onecote
Near Leek
Staffs ST13 7RW
Telephone (05388) 300

LEDA produce the *Sundomus* and the *Ion Drive* ionizers. Both these ionizers conform to BS 3456, and are in the lower price range although the quality is high. The Ion Drive uses a rotor to discharge the negative ions, and this has the advantage of avoiding any loss of ions due to absorption by plastic casing. LEDA will answer written or telephone enquiries.

Medion

P.O. Box 557
New Milton
Hants BH25 5YF
Telephone (0425) 638 205

Medion have a full range of air ionizers for the home, office, and car, including the international ionizer which is portable, and will run on any mains voltage in the world, or batteries. Some models have an on/off switch on the unit. Also included in their range of products are grille ionizers which fit over existing ventilation grilles, and atmospheric ion analysers for survey work. Medion will answer written or telephone enquiries.

Mountain Breeze
Peel House
Peel Road
Skelmersdale
Lancashire WN8 9PT
Telephone (0695) 21155

Mountain Breeze have a full range of room ionizers, a car ionizer, commercial and domestic air processing systems, and ion probes which are for use in homes, animal and bird enclosures, greenhouses, and workshops. Conforms to BS 3456 safety standard. Mountain Breeze will answer telephone and written enquiries.

Oasis Ltd
P.O. Box 74
Poole
Dorset BH15 2DZ
Telephone (0202) 672423

Oasis carry a full range of ionizers including a home, car, and commercial range. Conforms to BS 3456 safety standard. The Oasis room model has a fuse at the back of the appliance and includes an on/off button on the unit. Oasis will send information on request.

SKIN BRUSHES — VEGETABLE FIBRE

Green Farm Nutrition Centre
Burwash Common
East Sussex TN19 7LX
Telephone orders (0435) 882482 and 883457

You can also obtain other specialized personal items and supplements from Green Farm. Write to them for a catalogue.

USA:
Bernard Jensen Products
Solona Beach
CA 92075

Other brands of skin brushes are also generally available from most health stores.

VACUUM CLEANER

Vorwerk UK Ltd
Vorwerk House
Toutley Road
Wokingham
Berks RG11 5QN
Telephone (0734) 794878
Commercial Manager: James McAuley

Vorwerk USA
222 West Monte Drive South
Altamonte Springs
Florida, 32714-4257
Telephone (407) 682-2255

This is the most efficient vacuum cleaner for removing dust and its attendant problems, and is recommended by the Asthma Society. It removes the deep-seated dust and dirt that remains in furniture, carpets, and bedding. The Vorwerk vacuum cleaner also removes the grit from carpets that damages carpet fibres, but is not picked up by regular vacuum cleaners. It is particularly recommended for, and by, allergy and asthma sufferers. Contact Vorwerk if you would like to arrange a demonstration, of if you have any questions you would like answered.

INDEX